Sociodrama and Collective Trauma

Sociodrama
and Collective Trauma

Peter Felix Kellermann

Jessica Kingsley Publishers
London and Philadelphia

First published in 2007
by Jessica Kingsley Publishers
116 Pentonville Road
London N1 9JB, UK
and
400 Market Street, Suite 400
Philadelphia, PA 19106, USA

www.jkp.com

Library of Congress Cataloging in Publication Data

Kellermann, Peter Felix.
  Sociodrama and collective trauma / Peter Felix Kellermann.
    p. ; cm.
  Includes bibliographical references and index.
  ISBN-13: 978-1-84310-446-9 (pb)
  ISBN-10: 1-84310-446-6 (pb)
    1. Psychic trauma--Social aspects. 2. Post-traumatic stress disorder--Social aspects. 3. Sociodrama. I. Title.
    [DNLM: 1. Psychodrama--methods. 2. Stress Disorders, Post-Traumatic--therapy. WM 430.5.P8 K29s 2007]
  RC552.P67K442 2007
  362.196'8521--dc22
                                                    2006100118

British Library Cataloguing in Publication Data
A CIP catalogue record for this book is available from the British Library

ISBN 978 1 84310 446 9

Printed and bound in the United States of America by Thomson-Shore, Inc.

Contents

Acknowledgement

I would like to thank Allan Borowski for his help in editing some of the chapters of this book.

The author would like to receive correspondence on the following email address: natank@netmedia.net.il

Introduction

In his book, *Civilization and Its Discontents* (1930), Freud wrote:

> We are threatened with suffering from three directions: from our own body, which is doomed to decay and dissolution and which cannot even do without pain and anxiety as warning signals; from the external world, which may rage against us with overwhelming and merciless forces of destruction; and finally from our relations to other men. The suffering which comes from this last source is perhaps more painful to us than any other. (Freud 1930, p.77)

And the pain of human relations, to which Freud refers, is plentiful…

The pain from such wounds, inflicted by human beings upon one another, remains for a long time. It leads to trauma that is not only individual but also collective.

The purpose of this book is to describe such collective manifestations of trauma and how sociodrama may be used with groups that struggle with the after-effects of wars and natural disasters. More than anything else, however, it is an effort to share some thoughts and concerns, gleaned over a period of more than 30 years, from leading psychodrama and sociodrama groups in various parts of the world. Having worked with a large number and variety of trauma survivors, I started to discern a pattern that transcended the individuals and groups that I met. For instance, a woman described how she had recently lost three close female friends to cancer. In the psychodrama, group members, as usual, took the roles of the three women; the woman placed them side by side on the stage. As I looked at the three ladies sitting together and listened to the woman say farewell to each one of them in turn, I saw not only this individual loss and these few victims of cancer but also the thousands of similar victims of this and other fatal illnesses, and I felt the collective suffering of all the families and friends who were also mourning the deaths of their loved ones. Pursuing this imaginary encounter with the victims, I heard them ask questions that I could not answer: "Why did we die from this disease?", "Could it have been prevented?", "What is common among us?" I thought that, if I were only able to look at them carefully enough, I would perhaps discover their common secret and we would be able to prevent further casualties.

In my journeys throughout the world and in my work in Israel, I see such ghosts of the past everywhere, and they ask me similar questions: "Why did we die?", "Could it have been prevented?", "What is common among us?" I meet these victims through the numerous trauma survivors who present their life histories in psychodrama sessions and we invite them back in sociodrama. We encourage them to tell us what happened to them. Repeatedly, they talk about their collective trauma and ask if it was really inevitable or if it could have been prevented. I have often asked myself if I am crazy for hearing such things or if I am simply vicariously traumatized. Perhaps I am projecting my own unconscious fears upon these people or my own unfinished grief, or perhaps I am simply too sensitive to the suffering of people. Whatever the reason, I have come to realize that there is a common denominator in my work that centers on the themes of trauma, war, terror, disaster, and human suffering.

Human suffering as a result of disaster is no longer a remote phenomenon. On the contrary, it is one with which most of us have had direct or indirect contact. Many of us have experienced massive tragedy ourselves while others know someone who has been affected. With the global media coverage of today, all of us have seen disasters from afar on a daily basis and have sometimes visited disaster areas after catastrophic events have occurred. We have, therefore, become more than familiar with the features and details of disaster. For some of us, such events have started to convey some profound meaning and to hold some hidden significance. It is the aim of future sociodrama sessions to uncover this hidden meaning.

My first book, *Focus on Psychodrama* (1992), presented a systematic analysis of the essential therapeutic aspects of psychodrama. The second book, *Psychodrama with Trauma Survivors* (2000), edited together with Kate Hudgins, described the use of psychodrama with survivors of torture, war-related trauma, bereavement, addiction, and sexual abuse. Then I wrote a series of papers (Kellermann 2001a, 2001b, 2001c, 2001d) that dealt with the long-term effects of Holocaust trauma and its transmission to the second generation. These papers were based on my clinical and research experience from working as a clinical psychologist in a treatment center for Holocaust survivors and their children.

The present book is a natural continuation of this previous work. It is also a major revision and an extension of two previously published articles on interpersonal conflict management (Kellermann 1996) and sociodrama (Kellermann 1998). Both were published in *Group Analysis* and are here reprinted with permission. However, by emphasizing the psychological, social, political, cultural, and historical determinants of human behavior, the present book attempts to provide a perspective that is not only therapeutic but also sociopolitical. Perhaps it is, therefore, also preventive in its perspective. In other words, rather than only continuing to provide psychotherapy to individual trauma survivors, I have also found it increasingly important to discover how these events came to occur in the first place and to search for ways in which we can deal with them as a social group phenomenon.

Major traumatic events, such as war, terrorist bombings, and natural disasters, transcend the realms of individual suffering and enter the universal and collective sphere. Efforts to support individual trauma survivors and to alleviate community stress are complementary because major terrorist attacks around the world have taught us that we are all in this together. There can be no complete healing for anyone as long as the collective sources of trauma remain unaddressed because, in the long run, collective trauma cannot be healed as isolated events in the lives of individuals. It needs a group setting for its proper exploration and resolution.

Such a group setting will immediately make it obvious that people are influenced not only by their individual experiences, internal conflicts, and personality development but also by disastrous external sociopolitical realities, which are common to all. Psychotherapists who prefer to work within a social vacuum and who are blind to the external world neglect to acknowledge the fact that some clients simply respond in a normal manner to abnormal situations. These therapists run the danger of helping patients to adjust to a destructive society. As an illustration of this danger, O'Connor (1989) told the story of a young woman with symptoms of anxiety who came to Frieda Fromm-Reichmann for help in Europe before the Second World War, shortly before the therapist left for the United States. During the course of the psychoanalysis, the patient gradually overcame her fears, and after three years the therapy was successfully concluded. A few weeks later, however, the young woman, who was Jewish, was taken by the Gestapo and sent to a concentration camp.

This has been a difficult lesson to learn for many psychotherapists. As Sprague (1998) pointed out, "Every healer or therapist learns, sooner or later, the contradiction of helping people toward recovery and then sending them back into the conditions that made them ill in the first place" (p.250). Fortunately, group therapists today are in general deeply engaged in the sociopolitical realities of their countries and continually emphasize the influence of external factors on groups (e.g. Hearst 1993; Hopper 2002). Rather than focusing only on people in relation to themselves or in relation to a few others, group therapists often take a global view of intergroup and "group-as-a-whole" phenomena, keeping in mind the relation of one set of people to other people and to the society at large.

A highly potent but relatively unknown method for such group-as-a-whole explorations of the community at large is sociodrama. In sociodrama, people are invited to share their social concerns with one another. In addition, they are encouraged to develop community support networks that may strengthen the resilience of the population at large. The hope is that this will enable them to understand better why man-made violence occurs and to find more effective methods to manage conflicts between people and societies.

Until recently, a book such as this would be difficult to categorize within a specific academic field. It covers phenomena from sociology, social and clinical psychology, cultural anthropology, political science, and history. Osama bin Laden changed all that. The terrorist attack of September 11 2001 taught us that an interdisciplinary approach is required to understand today's global conflicts. Because the need is to heal the emotional wounds of the global human community as a whole, such an interdisciplinary approach should be better in dealing both with the many survivors and with the various levels of microsociological and macrosociological aspects, as well as in learning from history to prevent or to prepare us for future disasters.

We also need a broad-based approach to deal with conflict transformation, peace building, and the preparation or prevention of future conflict. The net effect would blur the boundary lines between the various subdisciplines. Clinical psychologists who work with groups could apply their diagnostic and therapeutic skills in sociopolitical settings; social psychologists could provide their knowledge of social influence, leadership, and mass communication to present-day global conflicts. Sociologists could add their cumulated data on the social lives of individuals, groups, and societies and the interactions between them; historians could put all this into a perspective of the past record of human societies. Anthropologists could make the relevant crosscultural comparisons; political scientists could try to integrate this vast material into their own analysis of political systems and behavior, international relations, and public policy and suggest relevant and effective approaches of intervention. Optimally, sociodrama could add to all this accumulated knowledge and draw upon all these fields of research. In addition, it also reflects upon morals, economics, government, religion, and the law and upon whatever is relevant for the problematic theme of a certain sociodrama group. Because all these factors are so interrelated, a perspective that puts the focus solely on one level is limited and incomplete.

This is perhaps a greater task than anyone ought to attempt because it implies a range of knowledge that many sociodramatists are painfully aware they do not possess. They may have some professional knowledge of psychological trauma and some clinical experience as psychotherapists, but there will always be much within all the other relevant fields of exploration about which they do not know enough.

In addition to these limitations, sociodramatists cannot claim any impartiality regarding the various themes and issues that are raised. Being "children of their times," they are faced with being deeply involved in the situations presented. Individuals cannot stand apart from their own nationalities, social classes, values, political convictions, and cultural backgrounds; these will, of course, immediately become apparent and interfere with their work. Thus, sociodramatists have no choice but to admit that their theories are themselves part of their personal points of view and of the social milieu in which they live. Taken as a whole, nothing said in sociodrama can therefore be said to be objectively right or wrong, true or false, or good or bad. The only thing we can be sure about is that everything said will include some personal valuations and predilections and, possibly, a fair amount of prejudice. It is therefore important to keep an open mind when working with sociodrama and try regularly to reevaluate sessions from the prism of various historical perspectives.

This pluralistic attitude may be a main reason for the aspiration of many sociodramatists and large-group leaders, including Moreno, to become citizens of the world rather than ethnocentric and proud representatives of one specific country. By not being directly affiliated to one specific country and to one specific cultural nationalism, one will identify with a larger variety of nationalities and ethnic tribes more easily and will adopt a kind of pluralistic identity.

From this combined personal, pluralistic, and probably biased perspective, I would like to provide some basic information about the author of this book. Much of this can be summarized by the various names that I have been given or that I later took and that more or less summarize the various cultural roles that I have adopted in the countries in which I have lived and worked.

Nama karana (a Zoroastrian term) or "giving a name to the child" (baptism, christening, etc.) is an important, almost sacred, ceremony in cultures around the world. It is a rite of passage that gives recognition and acceptance to a child as being the son or daughter of the father; until the ceremony is done and the father has accepted and named the child, the child is not fully accepted into the family and into the tribe. Giving a name to someone is like telling them who they are for the outer world. It is also a cultural marker that helps the child become integrated more easily into the specific society in which the family lives. Possibly much of it is based on the simple principle of assimilation, helping the child to become accepted and anchored into the local tribe and the immediate community. Taking a name later in life may, contrariwise, be an act of self-demarcation and individuation and an effort to adopt a different or an additional cultural role.

My grandparents were Jews from Eastern and Central Europe, and I received the name of Marcus after my great grandfather, who lived during the Austrian-Hungarian Empire. After the Second World War, my parents, who survived the Holocaust, found rescue and safe haven in Sweden, where I was born and grew up. To become a "real Swede" and help me meld into Swedish society as much as possible, I was given the name Peter. Two years earlier, my older brother had received the name Gustav, after the Swedish king. After immigrating to Israel in 1980, I became Natan, the mainstream Israeli Jew. None of these names ever "rubbed off" on me, and I still feel a peculiar sense of estrangement when people refer to me by these names. Therefore, when training in psychodrama at the Moreno Institute in the US, I took the international name of Felix to underline the flexible and spontaneous part of the roles I play in life.

As a result of this personal history of acculturation, I have become a little Austrian-Hungarian, Swedish, and Israeli. In addition, I am also an outsider in all countries because I do not really belong exclusively to any of them. Depending on the language I speak, I may feel more or less at home in one or the other country. When speaking German, for example, I feel a little Austrian; when speaking Swedish, I feel Swedish; and, when I speak Hebrew, I feel that I am Israeli. Rather than looking at these parts of myself merely as many identities that are in conflict with one another, I have come to view them as enriching experiences that help me to be in deep touch with these different cultures. Each name is the overt depiction or manifestation of these different cultural identities. As a whole, there is a real mix of cultural roles, each with its own interpersonal network and its often contradictory behavioral manifestations.

To go one step further in the process of role expansion, I have also intentionally experimented with the adaptation of more cultural identities through taking additional new names in different countries in which I have worked and visited. For example, in Turkey, I was given the Muslim name Nĕdím, which immediately made me feel more able to identify with the cultural roles of this country. In South Africa, I took the local name Aba Sali Bethu, trying to imagine how it would be to become a part of the indigenous Zulu tribe.

Such name-taking and -giving is more than merely imaginary role-taking and -playing. It is an intentional, partly intuitive, and almost anthropological effort to come as close as possible to a different culture to understand people of that culture from within. It is as if I want to become one of them, even if it is only through a virtual name and for a limited time, to get a real feeling for how it is to belong to their tribe. Only then will it be possible to get some actual feeling for the unique generalized characteristics of that people. As a result, it might also help me become more in tune with their historic struggles, feel their national grief, admire their national heroes, and let their collective unconscious shadows touch my heart.

This, I believe, is the essence of the struggle of any sociodramatist. Throughout this book and in future sociodrama sessions, you are also invited to share in this imaginary cultural role-taking.

1

Sociodrama

The true subject of a sociodrama is the group.

(Moreno 1953, p.88)

Sociodrama is an experiential group-as-a-whole procedure for social exploration and intergroup conflict transformation. J. L. Moreno, the founder of psychodrama and sociometry, developed this method during and after the
Second World War to improve the delicate fabric of coexistence between
various groups of postwar society.

In contrast to psychodrama, which focuses on individual dynamics, and
sociometry, the method for studying interpersonal relations, sociodrama was
developed as a deep action method for dealing with intergroup relations and
collective ideologies (Moreno 1943/1972). According to Moreno and
Moreno (1969):

> The difference between psychodrama and sociodrama is one of structure
> and objective. Psychodrama deals with a problem in which a single indi-
> vidual or a group of individuals are *privately* involved. Whereas
> sociodrama deals with problems in which the collective aspect of the
> problem is put in the foreground, the individual's private relation is put
> in the background. The two cannot, of course, be neatly separated.
> (p.270)

Sociodrama may be simply defined as a group method in which common
experiences are shared in action. It is the application of psychodrama techniques to social situations in the community. "As soon as the individuals are
treated as collective representations of community roles and role relations and
not as to their private roles and role relations, the psychodrama turns into a
'socio-psychodrama' or short sociodrama" (Moreno 1972, p.325).

In her review of the development of sociodrama in German-speaking countries, Geisler (2005) described the various corresponding approaches, such as group-centered or theme-centered psychodrama, pedagogical role-play, system-play, axiodrama, bibliodrama, large-group workshops, political stage, and the living newspaper. In her view, sociodrama is the overall concept of these approaches, succinctly defined as "the method that presents a theme with theatrical means" (p.158).

For example, a group may be enacting a terrorist attack in which various group members take the roles of the suicide bomber, the victims, the survivors, the emergency personnel, the politicians, the media, and the general bystander public. Another group may focus on the war in Iraq and personify the various principal actors in this conflict, including a dialogue between Saddam Hussein and George Bush. Any other social, political, or historical topic that engages the participants at a particular time may be dramatized and become a subject of the sociodrama.

Moreno hoped that, by reenacting intergroup conflicts and by having representatives of different groups reverse roles with one another, people could gain a perspective that would bring about understanding, peace, and a new social order (Marineau 1989). Gradually, he formulated a grand vision of improving intercultural relations around the world by conducting public sociodrama sessions that could be recorded and transmitted through mass media to millions of people.

Apart from his first sociodrama experiment in Vienna in 1921 and the living newspaper performances in the United States some ten years later, Moreno used sociodrama at professional meetings with mass audiences to explore a number of major social events, such as the Eichmann trial, the Kennedy assassination, and the Harlem riots, to mention but a few (Z. Moreno as cited in Sternberg and Garcia 1989). Sociodrama was later applied to various intergroup conflicts, such as those present in racially mixed areas, in law enforcement, and in education (Haas 1948). Monica Zuretti told the following story of a sociodrama in the United States:

> Many years ago, Moreno had a stage in New York where people could come in from the street and participate in an open psychodrama session. One evening, a young woman came up on stage and presented her predicament. She had just given birth to a beautiful child, but she was devastated, because the child was black, and her family did not accept it. She had fallen in love with a black man and they had married. At that time, inter-race marriages were unacceptable and large portions of society

would reject the couple and their children as well. As the session proceeded and the woman shared her concerns for the future of the small child, a woman from the audience appeared. By chance, she was a relative of the protagonist and had heard her cry for help. In a moving scene, she embraced the devastated mother and assured her that she would support them both, mindless of what their families felt. (Zuretti 2005, personal communication)

A complex mixture of internal and external factors influences the attitudes and behavior of human beings; and each sociodrama tries to uncover the broader social, political, economic, cultural, and religious determinants of a problem situation. In addition, it occurs within a specific historic context and the psychosocial situation of the participants.

Sociodrama sometimes appears similar to simple role-playing sessions, and some practitioners have looked down on its practice as superficial and impersonal and based too heavily on generalizations. While it is true that many of the role-playing activities allow participants to remain anonymous and/or to cover up their personal lives, the action can often be surprisingly emotional, touching upon themes about which people feel very strongly. In such instances, sociodrama becomes a profound human sharing experience, which is not inferior to psychodrama in terms of depth of experience. Carl Rogers' famous dictum that "What is most personal is most general" (the most private, personal feelings are often those which, if shared, would be most universal), may thus be paraphrased and stated in a contrariwise fashion: "What is most general is most personal."

Practice

In the first edition of their book *Sociodrama: Who's in Your Shoes?* Sternberg and Garcia (1989) described sociodrama as a variety of role-playing applications in education, business, therapy, and theater. As far as I understand it, these activities should be designed as theme-centered or group-centered psychodrama and not as sociodrama because the expressed goal of sociodrama is to explore social events and community patterns that transcend particular individuals. This includes especially the practices described in their chapter 14 and it has become more apparent in the fully revised second edition (Sternberg and Garcia 2000) in which they defined sociodrama as a group learning process. The goal of this process is to provide practice in solving problems of human relations through action while uncovering the commonalities among people, thus allowing the thoughts, feelings, and hopes of all participants to rise to the surface.

As mentioned in the recently published *Handbook Sociodrama: The Whole World on the Stage* edited by Wittinger (2005), two different schools of sociodrama seem to have evolved. The first – represented also in my present book – insists that sociodrama should deal only with the group as a whole, while the second school also includes a kind of (multiple) protagonist-centered or theme-centered approach on the condition that it looks at each individual person both as a bearer of collective roles and as a representative of the common themes of the entire group. Both positions base themselves on Moreno's earlier work, which switched from one emphasis to the other. Perhaps this is one reason Ron Wiener (1997) included both kinds of sociodrama in his teaching.

Though sociodrama may utilize familiar psychodramatic techniques, such as role reversal, doubling, mirroring, soliloquy, sculpturing, and general improvisational role-playing, it is my position that it is essentially different from psychodrama. This is because unlike psychodramatists, who are concerned with the responses of specific individuals to various situations, sociodramatists will try to understand human social behavior in general and focus on the group as a whole. The group as a whole is a basic postulate in sociodrama, according to Moreno (1943/1972). "It is the group as a whole, which has to be put upon the stage to work out its problem, because the group in sociodrama corresponds to the individual in psychodrama" (p.354). Thus, sociodrama can be regarded as an action-oriented counterpart to group analysis (Hamer 1990; Powell 1986).

By focusing on groups and societies, sociodrama is a form of "socio-therapy" rather than a form of psychotherapy, which focuses on the personalities of individual members, including their roles. To put it simply, a psychodramatist looks at each tree one at a time while a sociodramatist insists on seeing the entire forest.

The following example may illustrate this collective perspective. An envious husband recently murdered a female colleague of mine, leaving their two children without parents. During this same week, three more women were also murdered by their male partners for similar reasons. Most people only looked at each individual catastrophe, expressing their feelings of grief, despair, and outrage at each specific tragedy, regarded as an exceptional phenomenon. Few saw the general trend of violence in our society against women, against weak groups, and against minorities. Many were either unwilling or almost incapable of understanding that such tragedies may have been caused not only by the individual disturbances of these violent men but also by the norms and attitudes prevalent in our society as a whole.

This sociodramatic perspective is based on the generalizing function of people, described in detail by Gestalt psychology. It sees the brain as a holistic, self-organizing, and formative entity that enables people to learn how to recognize figures and whole forms instead of just a collection of simple lines and curves. This "Gestalt effect" provides the skill to generalize a whole from a compilation of separate details. In sociodrama, this ability is used to discern the general effect of a series of events, which were originally not contained in the sum of the parts. As in a motion picture, we slowly start to understand the developing story from looking at the compilations of thousands of individual lights, pictures, and scenes, which originally had no apparent connection between them. Similarly, the sociodramatic narrative is developed gradually as we come to recognize some of the various relationships among the single events and succeed in binding them together into a coherent whole.

Setting and process

From a technical point of view, sociodrama is ideally conducted in a large hall with movable chairs or in an open amphitheatre or a town square with suitable sound amplification equipment. People sit around an open empty space in the middle where the action takes place under the leadership of a sociodramatist who tries to keep the group focused and actively involved.

The approximate timeframe for a sociodrama session varies from one-and-a-half to two-and-a-half hours but may also continue for a day or more with some breaks in between sessions.

The group should be as heterogeneous as possible to represent the actual population at large. The size of group varies from a minimum of 20 to 40 participants to 40 to 80 through large groups of 100 or more to very large groups of 1000 people at some international congresses.

The size of a sociodrama group has a significant effect on the group process, and specific large-group dynamics should be taken into account when practicing sociodrama. Large groups are characterized by various projective processes, depersonalization and personality invasion, anonymization and generalization, envy, and "forced" democratization (Agazarian and Carter 1993; de Maré, Piper and Thompson 1991; Klein 1993; Kreeger 1975; Main 1975; Milgram and Toch 1969; Schneider and Weinberg 2003; Seel 2001).

Most powerful is the extraordinarily high interpersonal energy level of the large group, as if the "crowd" has a life of its own, which in itself creates an extraordinary environment for intergroup explorations.

Facilitating such a mass of people within one setting is a formidable task not suitable for any one person. Just keeping track of all the different people who want to say something or become actively involved is a difficult job. If possible, it may therefore be wise to work with a team that can plan the session before it starts, assist the process during the action, and make some kind of postsession evaluation after it has ended. Such a team is important in helping the group process move through the phases of sociodrama more smoothly. While still led by one sociodrama leader, the team members can also provide individual support if needed, follow participants who leave the room to ensure that they are okay, help silent members communicate their feelings, and suggest possible avenues for continuation when the process gets stuck. A handful of such team members in each session, who are introduced to the group at the beginning of the session, can make a substantial difference in the successful completion of the sociodramatic group process. In addition, the very cooperation between the team members and the sociodramatist may in itself be a good learning experience for the participants, who will see in action how the group as a whole is more than the sum of each separate part.

When working in large groups, it is helpful to have a wireless microphone, which can be passed from one participant to the other so that everyone can hear what is said. This is an important technical aid to the group that also creates some structure in the process, allowing one person at a time to talk.

The ambition of the sociodramatist should be to let as many individuals as possible say something to the entire group. This is not only important from a technical point of view. It conveys the message that every individual person is important in this group and that every voice can really be heard. In my experience, there is a kind of relief in the tension of the group when this happens, as if it conveys some basic feeling of equality that counteracts a hierarchical power structure. The larger the group, the greater is the relief. This is because it is a manifestation of democracy and pluralism in action. It also conveys a kind of counter-message to "group mentality" and group pressure because it permits each individual to be different.

Sociodramatist skills

Naturally, handling large numbers of people who struggle with intergroup social conflicts is not an easy task. Not only is it difficult to keep the boundaries and hold everything together, but group facilitators and sociodramatists also face some inherent pitfalls that demand special attention to prevent psychological casualties. First, if hostilities are expressed, subgroups may become unrestrained herds that inflict harm on one another and/or on the sociodramatist. Second, charismatic and power-hungry leaders may use the large group for their own narcissistic needs rather than for empowering others and thus create an authoritarian mass marathon psychology organization (Cushman 1989) that has a repressive influence on people. Third, intense uncontrolled emotions may be evoked without sufficient small-group network support available, leaving people lonely and vulnerable. Finally, sociodrama may appear too simplistic, too superficial, too sentimental, and too optimistic about the possibility of peaceful coexistence (Sabelli 1990) if practiced in an unrealistic and naive manner.

Therefore, apart from the necessary knowledge and skills, sociodramatists also need to have much courage, stature, and experience to do the job effectively. While being sufficiently confident to enter the sociopolitical scene, they should also know their specific areas of competence and not be afraid to decline a group because it exceeds their limitations. Still, it is important to meet every group with a sense of awe, privilege, and enthusiasm.

In addition to these requirements, one needs to be well-informed about world affairs to do this work well. Sociodramatists should at least attempt to be well-informed about the specific recent and past history of the country and community in which they are working. Without such knowledge, they will be unable to comprehend the narratives of the participants and be at a loss about possible ways to proceed with an exploration of collective past history. It is therefore important that sociodramatists assemble basic information about past and recent events that affected the people before conducting the group. Only then will they be able to stage and dramatize such significant events properly. Naturally, it is impossible to learn about all the historical and sociopolitical details. Some will be learned as the work proceeds and through the information provided by the participants, but there will also be basic facts that participants will not mention and that will remain hidden if the director does not get the information before the group. This especially concerns perspectives in a conflict in which both parties neglect to talk about their own aggressions and only focus on the misbehavior of the other side and on themselves as the victims.

From all the assembled information, the sociodramatist will try to formulate a shared central issue on which the group can focus during the sociodrama. The formulation of such a central and shared issue may or may not coincide with the group's conscious motive for coming together. While there may be other concerns that the group wants to explore, the director needs to find a way to explain the relevance of the issue to the group and to put the group in a situation in which facing themselves means facing their past. A helpful sign that the central issue is correctly chosen is that the group is emotionally moved by the theme and that the participants seem to be interested in sharing their own perspectives and personal concerns about it.

If the central issue is agreed upon, the sociodramatist makes a statement that acknowledges, verbalizes, and summarizes it to the group. Similar to a treatment contract negotiated in time-limited psychotherapy, sociodramatists will base this statement on their understanding of the psychosocial determinants of a specific community. There will be some reference to something tragic that happened in the past, which also remains active in most group members in the present and which is still resonating in its collective unconscious. In addition, the statement may include both the mastering and defensive efforts of the community in responding to the event. For example, after the earthquake in Turkey, the director might say:

> We found the earthquake overwhelming. We were scared to death. Everything was out of control. We searched for the best ways to master the difficulties. But then it became too much, and we simply tried to forget about it and put it out of our minds and continued as if nothing had happened. But when we see the destruction, we start to remember. It still hurts. Let's look at it together.

During the enactment of the scene, there is much freedom for the various actors to perform the roles they play as they like. Other group members may also suddenly step in and add a sentence or take over the dialogue altogether. As we learn about the entire situation, new characters are introduced and the action develops spontaneously with minimal restrictions. At some strategic points, the director may ask leading questions so that the narrative is developed and the group can move forward.

Drawing on cultural anthropology and utilizing techniques from group and family systems therapy, as well as actively utilizing the standard

techniques of psychodrama and role-playing, sociodrama attempts to combine these approaches into a single, cohesive method. In any sociodrama,
some or all of the major techniques of psychodrama (role reversal, doubling,
mirroring, soliloquy, and concretization) may be adapted to the special needs
of a specific group. If, for example, the group consists of traumatized people
who have all survived the same tragic experience, the group leader may want
to evaluate their varying degrees of "learned helplessness," the feeling that
their destiny is shaped by external forces over which they have no control. In
such a case and if the session is held early after the actual disaster, the doubling
technique may be used for "containing" emotions (Hudgins and Drucker
1998) rather than for unrestrained abreaction. The mirror technique may also
be used to help the group get some detachment and some distance from the
frightening event.

At the end of the action, there should be some time left for closure. This
final stage provides an ending to the exploration and a sense of completion in
the group. Culturally appropriate rituals (Kellermann 1992) may be used to
dramatize such endings. As a matter of principle, there should also be plenty
of time for verbal sharing after each sociodrama. These expressions may be
more or less personal, according to the theme that was explored. There are
some instances in which impersonal issues, including political actions, are also
suggested in such postaction sharing. Contrary to the rules of strictly personal
sharing in psychodrama, it is my view that these comments may be allowed
and even encouraged after a sociodrama session.

Sociodrama around the world

2005 was a very difficult year. Violent conflicts and natural disasters affected
many people throughout the world. Sociodrama was increasingly applied to
assist the survivors of such tragedies.

A few years earlier, Bradshaw-Tauvon (2001) had reflected on the use of
sociodrama for peace building within local, regional, and international con-
ferences in the UK, Sweden, and Israel. She wrote that these settings provided
a marvelous forum to bring together diverse cultures for the exploration of
social issues. She described how sociodrama can be used to nurture genuine
encounters between individuals and small groups and to create ways to effect
constructive change in and between societies, cultures, and countries. In an
example from Norway (Lillian Borge), she recounted a sociodrama that
focused on the pain, sorrow, and guilt experienced by young men who

participate in war. After exploring the various issues involved in major violent conflicts, the group came to the tragic conclusion that it was impossible, at that time, to build a bridge between the conflicting parties because one side of the conflict refused to cooperate. Lillian Borge, quoted in Bradshaw-Tauvon, said, "The sorrow concerned not being able to reach across gaps, sorrow about having to accept how difficult building bridges is, whether it is a question of global politics or psychotherapeutic methods" (2001, p.25).

Such peace-promoting activities have become a common and recurring theme in many congresses of the International Association of Group Psycho- therapy (IAGP) during the last few decades. For example, there was an ongoing large group with about 150 participants led by both Marcia Karp, who was using sociodrama, and by Theresa Howard, who used group analysis, during the fourteenth IAGP congress in Jerusalem in August 2000 with the theme "From Conflict to Generative Dialogue."

During this Jerusalem conference, a symbolic wall was depicted in various group sessions. It appeared in the words and associations of participants during large group sessions and during the various workshops conducted before and during the congress. The wall evoked strong emotions and seemed to concretize the interpersonal tensions between the various subgroups present. In addition to its symbolic significance, it had also been introduced by the program planning committee, which had intentionally kept the two daily large group sessions apart from one another by a closed (but mobile) wall so that there was never an open setting in which the entire group of partici- pants could interact. Perhaps the committee conceived this separation of groups as a viable solution to the intergroup tensions that appeared. Bradshaw-Tauvon (2001), who was present during the dramatization of this wall in one of the groups, described the various emotional responses of the group:

> For some it is relief, for others a frustration. It is related to as inevitable, necessary, an obstacle, as representative of inner walls. The wall in the large group for many is experienced as a barrier, even if for many it is a protection. At first the wall is built of men and women, but the men quickly leave. Later it becomes a protective surrounding wall with a man in the center. The changing images are very strong and do much to elucidate the processes in this group which contains people from 38 different countries, Armenians, Christians, Moslems, Jews, non- believers, various professionals, the categories that divide us are too many to mention. What unites us is the struggle to communicate authen-

tically in a larger setting on a human, socio-political level and the struggle to accept each other with all our differences where every voice and action is important. (p.27)

As a permanent resident of Jerusalem and a citizen of Israel, I felt that creating and maintaining this artificial barrier between the two large groups was very destructive. In fact, it was a blow in the face to anyone who had hitherto believed in the power of dialogue to resolve conflicts. Despite my repeated outrage and protests in both large group sessions, there seemed to be little understanding of my point of view at that time.

About a month later, the recent Intifada started in Israel and has since then resulted in thousands of innocent victims on both sides of the conflict. After scores of suicide bombings and daily terrorist attacks against its civilians, Israel's unity government decided to construct a security fence between Israel and the West Bank to prevent Palestinian terrorists from infiltrating Israeli population centers. The project has had the overwhelming support of the Israeli public, which sees the barrier as vital to their security. The same separation wall is perceived by the Palestinians as a land grab, a prison wall, and an act of racism.

As well as filling the physical separation function for all neighboring peoples, any "wall" is also a powerful symbol of psychological demarcation. Volkan (2002) discussed this function in his paper on border psychology as it pertained to German reunification. Observing how a physical border can act as a kind of psychological skin around large-group identities, Volkan noticed that, when taken away, this border would force both groups to redefine their own identities. To maintain their own distinct group identities, both East and West Germany would suddenly become aware of their need to maintain some kind of clear psychological border between them. Such an inner, imaginary border is often projected upon the political (or physical) border or, as in the case of the international congress, upon any movable wall between different groups.

I do not understand the full significance of the above events and do not want to imply that the IAGP congress caused the recent Intifada. Despite the fact that a war also broke out in the former Yugoslavia a few years after the IAGP congress in Zagreb in 1986, there are certainly sufficient other reasons for such military tensions, without the infighting of a few group psychotherapists. What I want to emphasize is only the connection between the symbolic manifestation of a wall within the groups and the actual historic building of a security fence in the country in which the groups met. Apparently, the groups were a true reflection (or a microcosm) of the society in which they occurred. As such, they conveyed profound wisdom because, if we become aware of such physical and psychological demarcations, we may be able to facilitate change that goes beyond the intrapsychic and interpersonal disturbances of our clients and affects intergroup tensions on a global scale. This is perhaps one of the humble goals of sociodrama.

In the aftermath of every catastrophic event, sociodramatists may be called upon to assist the many groups of people who are affected. In such situations, sociodrama has much to offer not only to the individual survivors and to their families but also to entire communities that struggle to come to terms with what they have experienced.

Various forms of such sociodrama sessions have been applied to major international catastrophic events (Knepler 1970). One of the most well known is perhaps the sociodrama with the anguished people of Argentina during the military junta and later during the Falklands War (Bustos 1994). In England, Ken Sprague and Marcia Karp worked with people on the other side of this conflict. Other examples of sociodrama include Ella-Mae Shearon's work on the German election of right-wing extremists in 1989 (Feldhendler 1994) and the explorations of the sociopolitical realities in Paraguay (Carvalho and Otero 1994). A recent handbook on sociodrama in German was edited by Wittinger (2005) with a series of relevant applications and developments, showing that the field is still growing in scope.

The second edition of Sternberg and Garcia's (2000) book *Sociodrama: Who's in Your Shoes?* includes several other examples of sociodrama in English-speaking countries. Accounts of some sessions conducted in Eastern Europe during the great transition are described in the German journal *Psychodrama* (e.g. Lobeck 1990; Zichy 1990), and Stein, Ingersoll and Treadwell (1995) write about a sociodrama conducted during the Gulf War. Roman Solotowitzki in Moscow has been working and developing a sociodramatic institute that will focus on role reversal with the enemy. The Kiev *Psychodrama* Association published a series of papers on sociodrama in the Ukraine and Russia (Solotowitzki 2004). Ron Wiener (1997, 2001), who leads one of the few schools of sociodrama in the UK and organizes training in various countries, has utilized a sociodrama method combined with "creative training" in various parts of the world. An exploration of the Jewish–Arab conflict in Israel, including a reenactment of a terrorist bombing, was conducted at the International Psychodrama Conference in Jerusalem in 1996. On the other side of this conflict, Ursula Hauser, together with

Mohammed K. Mukhaimar, has been working with sociodrama under very difficult circumstances in the Gaza community mental health center for a number of years (Hess 2004).

In a special issue of the *Journal of the Yugoslav Psychodrama Association*, Djuric, Ilić, and Veljkovic (2004) reported on sociodrama workshops held during and after the 1999 war in Serbia in which Serbs endured 69 days of NATO bombing. In this same journal, Ilić (2004) shared his appreciation of being contacted by the international psychodrama community during this difficult time:

> At the end of March, I got an e-mail from P. F. Kellermann and he asked how we are and what is happening. It is as if someone sincerely asked you for your health, and you feel very bad, so we took our chance and opened our souls. It was a patriotic cry, an accusation and a need to awaken conscience, even pity, and testing friendliness... The letter was sent to a global psychodrama mailing list and after that and during the war we got many letters with questions, support, and just greetings. (p.88)

Among the many people who responded was Shirley Barclay from the US, who urged her Native American brothers and sisters from the Comanche tribe to pray and perform rituals within the overall therapeutic framework of *mitakuye oyasin* ("we are all related") for the victims of the air strikes. This had a profound effect on the Serbian group that had earlier felt very isolated within the international community.

Possibly, collectivist cultures such as those common in Asia, Africa, South America, and the Pacific regions may be more open to sociodrama, while psychodrama may be more easily received in Western Europe and in North America, which have more individualistic cultures. In the former culture, people are used to subordinating their personal goals to those of the collective, while the latter is characterized by the primacy of individual rights and personal goals (Triandis *et al.* 1988).

Indeed, sociodrama seems to be suited to African culture and is also very popular in Latin America. In Africa, Gong Shu (2004), together with Jon Kirby, Edward Salifu Mahama, and Renee Oudijk from the Netherlands, worked with the Dagomba and the Konkomba tribes from Ghana in West Africa within a fascinating spiritual setting of cross-cultural sociodrama. In Managua, Geisler (2005) used a combination of sociodrama and bibliodrama on the revolution in Nicaragua. In addition, Mascarenhas described the use of the "dramatic multiplication" technique applied to social issues in a book on psychodrama in Brazil, called *Sambadrama* (Figusch 2006). In fact, Brazil has been the fertile ground for many innovative drama methods that have a decidedly sociopolitical emphasis. It will be interesting to see how this is going to be presented in the upcoming IAGP congress in Sao Paulo in 2006.

Marise Greeb in Sao Paulo organized one of the largest sociodrama events in the world on March 21 2000. Hundreds of public sociodrama, bibliodrama, and axiodrama sessions were held on the theme of citizenship and ethics. Adam Blatner reported that 700 psychodramatists directed sociodramas about issues in the life of the community in 180 locations in 96 city districts – indoors in libraries, schools, and other auditoriums and even outdoors in plazas – free and open to the public. An estimated 8000 citizens participated. The program lasted two to three hours. There were small and large groups, with 10 to 600 participants present at each sociodrama. Many people spoke about how powerful the experience was, for both the psychodramatists and the participants. Deep feelings of sadness were expressed, along with powerlessness, humiliation, sometimes happiness, and at the end of the sociodramas hope for better times. The mayor of Sao Paulo, Marta Suplicy, who supported this project and apparently has had some psychodrama training herself, participated in one of the scenes, taking the role of a victim of violence.

The late Ken Sprague from the United Kingdom was a true sociodramatist and a (nonviolent) revolutionary. From his own life history, he had a deep understanding of how society worked and he was devoted to promoting change whenever he saw that there was some injustice done. He argued for a method that was based upon the active involvement of people, not upon political institutions and controlling power. His untimely death was a big loss for our community. I loved his earnest and straightforward manner, and it was always obvious how much he cared about making the world a better place to live. His paper "Permission to interact: a who, how and why of sociodrama" is one of the finest texts on sociodrama that I know. In this paper, Sprague (1998) wrote:

> Our primary task is not to save the rainforests or stop fox hunting, although we may support such campaigns. Nor is it to preserve the birds and their breeding grounds, although these might be ideal themes for sociodramas. Our aim is to save our humanity, which is essential at this stage of evolution if all our other efforts are to succeed. (p.252)

Last, but not least, I would like to mention the extraordinary, important work of Monica Zuretti from Argentina. She has made a deep impact on thousands of people around the world and in many cultural settings. For example, in the slum of Villa Miseria, she worked with a group of mothers, some of whom were of native origin belonging to the tribes of La Pampa. These people lived according to a matriarchal social structure and based their lives on their relationship with Mother Earth (*Pacha Mama*). Perhaps Zuretti was correct in insisting that sociodrama and psychodrama cannot really be differentiated; she therefore developed a special combination method of "socio-psycho-drama" in which both the private and the collective (and the figure and ground) must be emphasized at different phases of the group process. Zuretti (2001) wrote:

> Sometimes the resolution of a sociodramatic scene could not be reached until, in the same group or in another, a protagonist incarnated the problem, worked on it, and gave the social matrix the possibility of change. Also, there was sometimes no possibility of understanding a personal situation, until it was related to the social environment. (p.111)

From this approach, Zuretti works with the personal histories of group members, as much as the relationships between those personal histories and the history and traumatic scenes of the social matrix. As the group develops, group members start to understand how their personal drama is also a part of the drama of humankind. In simple words, for Zuretti, everything is connected to everything else, although we do not always understand immediately how this connection is manifested. This is a beautiful and succinct way of describing the essence of sociodrama.

This work is developing in new directions, integrating findings from a variety of new sources. For example, Monica Westberg at the Swedish Psychodrama Academy conducted a sociodrama workshop with Johan Galtung (1996) and Monica Zuretti on peace building in the summer of 2006. In her paper "The psychodrama of mankind: is it really utopian?" Rosa Cukier (2000) from Sao Paulo, Brazil, was impressed not only by the breadth and depth of the various international applications of sociodrama but also by the sheer enthusiasm and profound courage of the practitioners to undertake such an enormous task. It seemed to her that many practitioners have been deeply influenced by Moreno's (1953) grandiose credo that "a truly therapeutic procedure cannot have less an objective than the whole of mankind" (p.698). She felt that Moreno's pretension to treat the whole of mankind always seemed exaggerated and improbable to her; but, after observing the important work done in various parts of the world, she concluded that psychodramatists seem to have the daring that it takes to push this social project forward.

Indeed, today there are practitioners all over the world dedicated to this universal agenda and, in a way, it has united the global psychodramatic family in a common purpose beyond the practice of protagonist-centered psychodrama. Whatever words we use to describe this agenda, it includes assisting various groups of people with their collective trauma to promote justice and equality and to develop new avenues for friendly coexistence.

Conclusion

Social gatherings of all the significant persons in our lives occur only on rare occasions. Normally, we celebrate milestones like births, graduations, and weddings and participate in funeral services together. These occasions provide opportunities for reunions in which the nuclear and extended family, friends, neighbors, and colleagues come together to celebrate, sharing food and spirits, in joy and sadness. Ethnic tribes, or people who have something in common, have always chosen to announce transitions in life or to acknowledge their new status during such public events. We have all experienced the dramatic power of being included in such gatherings, and they hold some special significance for us all through life.

While sociodrama sessions are convened for other purposes, they may hold similar significance for those who attend them. Whether the gathering follows a crisis or focuses on politics, diversity, conflict, or reconciliation in the school, the workplace, the church, or the neighborhood, the session often remains in our consciousness for a long time. Participants tend to appreciate the power of such a gathering and cherish its memory for a long time. It is as if the participation in itself acknowledges that we belong to a larger social network and it seems that, in a time of increasing alienation, such public events become more and more important for us.

Simply put, sociodrama provides an open stage, a setting, and a procedure in which various collective forces can be played out. In this setting, every participant is significant and regarded as a part of the whole. Their feelings, thoughts, and actions can be neither predicted nor controlled. In addition, whatever happens in the session doesn't follow strict rules, even though it is usually possible to discern the various phases of warm-up, action, closure, and sharing as they develop. These phases usually evolve in a spontaneous fashion and most sessions proceed differently from other sociodrama sessions.

2

Collective trauma

On April 26 1986, there was a massive explosion in the nuclear power plant at Chernobyl in the Ukraine. The blast killed at least 30 people and forced the evacuation of 135,000 citizens due to the high level of nuclear contamination in the area. However, the effects of the disaster were not limited to this area. A radioactive cloud swept across Belarus and Northern Europe; and, as a result, there has been a dramatic rise in the number of cases of thyroid cancer, leukemia, birth defects, and other health problems in these areas. Twenty years after the accident, it is estimated that more than 800 people in northern Sweden have developed cancer as a result of the radioactive fallout in this area. The long-term health effects may be even more far-reaching because even the smallest amounts of radioactive fallout can cause genetic damage that appears only in future generations. Overall, more than 6 million people may have been affected by the world's worst nuclear disaster (see Van den Bout, Havenaar and Meijler-Iljina 1995).

In 2005, when I visited Slavutych, a town built for the displaced population of Chernobyl, I could see for myself how the survivor population were still trying to recover and build new lives for themselves. The directly exposed adult survivors were regularly monitored for health risks, while children born many years after the accident were perpetually painting pictures of houses on fire.

This is the essence of collective trauma. Its profound after-effects are manifold and far-reaching.

Like a nuclear bomb that disperses its radioactive fallout in distant places even a long time after the actual explosion, any major psychological trauma continues to contaminate those who were exposed to it in one way or another in the first, second, and subsequent generations. Similar to radioactivity, the emotional trauma cannot be seen or detected. Perceived as being as dangerous as the radioactive substances that lie buried under the tons of concrete poured over the nuclear power plant at Chernobyl, collective trauma remains hidden in the dark abyss of the unconscious. While the degree of contagion may be less visible and may even diminish over time, there will always remain a trace of the blast imprinted upon the molested space of human consciousness. While on the surface things may look quite normal, the very absence of something that was there before – the void or empty space – will have a psychological effect on anyone who visits the disaster area and reveals its hidden secret.

Gampel (1996) introduced the concept of "radioactivity" in connection with the parental transmission of Holocaust trauma. This process seems to occur through a kind of "radioactive" leakage in which children of survivors start to internalize the incomprehensible fears and anxieties of their parents and become "contaminated" themselves as a result. Gampel (2000) used the term "radioactive identification," to describe:

> a conceptual and metaphoric representation of the penetrations of the terrible, violent, and destructive aspects of external reality against which the individual is defenceless. This radioactive identification or radioactive nucleus comprises non-representable remnants of the radioactive influence which cannot be spoken about or described in words but instead reveal themselves through images, nightmares, and symptoms. (p.59)

Collective trauma does not only contaminate people. It also leaves its traces on physical locations. In addition to the entire area of Chernobyl, examples of such contaminated places include Ground Zero in New York, traces of the former Berlin Wall, the Auschwitz concentration camp, and the empty shores of the December 26 2004 tsunami wave in the Far East. All these places have left their visible or invisible scars not only on the geography of the earth but also on the collective consciousness of the communities affected and of humankind in general. With a little imagination, one can still hear the desperate cries for help at these places. A place that has been hit seems to hold some mystical, cursed meaning for survivors. These places – or hotspots – become triggers that reactualize the traumatic event. In such places, the brain seems to send false alarms that there is some impending danger and, as a result, people mobilize themselves for self-protection. With or without memorial plaques, citizens remember for years where each tragedy took place and reexperience some of the terror when they visit those locations later. For example, the No. 30 bus that exploded in London became such a dreaded place that people tried to avoid it. Similarly, the underground, which had been the "safe place" during the London Blitz of the Second World War, later became "unsafe" during the IRA terrorist bombings and now even more so.

Decades and centuries after a disaster, the presence of trauma is felt not only by individual survivors and their families but also by people on the periphery who, although not directly hit, were nevertheless affected. For some, these effects may be almost inaudible, constituting only a disturbing background noise. For others, they are heard loud and clear and become a constant companion of irritating stress and anxiety; many of these people fear new tragedy for the rest of their lives.

An example of this tacit fear could be observed during a sociodrama workshop in the UK in which the Blitz, the intense bombing of the United Kingdom by Nazi Germany during 1940–1941, was reenacted. At that time, London was bombed during either the day or night and fires destroyed many parts of the city. Residents sought shelter wherever they could find it, many fleeing to the underground stations. The bombardment caused approximately 43,000 deaths and the destruction of over a million houses.

When hearing a recreation of the air raid sirens sounding, the airplanes coming, and the bombs falling over London, a woman in her sixties panicked. Her entire body shook as she vividly recalled this time from her childhood. She had been awakened at the commencement of the night raids and told to dress quickly and hurry to the cellar. As she was running to escape to the relative safety of the shelter, she dropped down on her knees at the corner of the room and put her hands over her ears. At that moment, we were all hearing the bombs falling and seeing the London horizon on fire. The past had been brought into the present and the entire group was in terror. At the end of the reenactment, someone finally stood up and declared the famous speech of Winston Churchill: "We shall fight on the beaches…we shall never surrender…" It helped us all to relax a little.

Many years later, terror returned to London. On July 12 2005 in the worst bombing attack since the Second World War, it was reminiscent of the Blitz; but this time the bombs were largely regarded as insignificant. In fact, most Londoners seemed to be less upset by the terrorist bombs than they had been after the death of Princess Diana. The media took note. Reporting this event on CNN, Charles Hudson observed that Londoners had shown less public expression of grief than the citizens of Madrid and New York after their terrorist bombings. Instead, he explained, the "bottled-up Brits" seemed to join forces in a unanimous effort to "play down" or "cover up" the psychological effects of the disaster and to keep much of their emotions to themselves.

There may be several explanations for this restrained reaction. Perhaps Londoners weren't all that worried because it was merely a "one-off" event without continuation. Another reason may be that the recent terrorist events evoked recollections not only of the Blitz and of the Second World War but also of much larger disasters in the ancient history of London, such as of the Great Plague of 1665–1666 that killed more than a third of London's population and of the Great Fire that followed immediately and destroyed most of the city. In addition, it may also have reactivated the memory of the Irish potato famine in which over a million people died of hunger at a time when Great Britain was one of the richest nations on earth. According to Sprague (1998), "We still suffer the consequences of that murderous period" (p.247). Compared with these ancient traumatic events, the 2005 terrorist bombing was apparently considered a minor disaster.

Clearly, any major traumatic event will continue to plague the various affected populations for generations. My own sociodrama work has repeatedly shown that a historical echo continues to reverberate in people from all over the world and that they have a need to share their collective grief and anguish in a manner that convinced me that the wounds remain open and unhealed for a very long time. During the last three decades, I have repeatedly observed such after-effects, manifested, for example, in the terrible consequences of the communist regime and the famine on the people in the Ukraine (and on the other countries in the former USSR, including Estonia and Latvia), the earthquakes in Turkey, the tensions between North and South Korea, the apartheid regime in South Africa, the nuclear bombs in Japan during the Second World War, the racial prejudices in the US, the Peninsular War in Spain and Portugal, Stalin's communist torture of the population in Sofia, Bulgaria, and the wars in Cyprus and in Israel.

In addition to these group experiences, I remember a sociodrama session in Torino with Maurizio Gasseau in which we observed how the ancient division of old Italy with all its local traditions and intergroup tensions was still an important part of Italian internal politics. In fact, the terrible long-term effects of the Second World War were apparent in most European countries (Holland, Belgium and France). From a different perspective, groups in Germany, Austria, and Italy dealt with the long-term effects of their National Socialist and fascist pasts on their national consciousness (Kellermann 2004).

When leading psycho- and sociodrama workshops in these countries, the sediments of such past tragedies constantly reappeared. It was as if the wars were still all around us, everywhere. Even in such a beautiful and tranquil place as the little town of Lillehammer in Norway, there were vivid memories of the Second World War, of the Quislings, victims, and bystanders. Similarly, the Finns shared their many years of famine and we clearly felt the present influence of the struggle of the ancient Swedish King Gustav Vasa in the little town of Mora during a recent summer seminar there.

This sociodrama work transcended simple role-playing reenactments of historic events: it had a stronger impact on people than the detached, sympathetic acknowledgement of tragic news watched on CNN. These were collective traumatic events to which the majority of the group could relate emotionally. We could all feel the death angst of the victims and the grief of the surviving families. What became apparent was that, when we faced this history together, we also faced some deep and often untouched parts of ourselves. In those moments, we became united around the commonalities of all of humankind, regardless of cultural heritage.

Collective traumatic events

Apparently, all collective traumas leave a dark shadow over the history of humankind.

Major traumatic events have occurred in countries all over the world, both in the recent past and in distant history. Such events may have been caused either by the forces of nature (floods, earthquakes, windstorms, famines, diseases, tsunamis, etc.) or intentionally by human beings (wars, terrorist bombings, genocides, etc.). In addition, there are unintentional man-made disasters, such as large fires, boat and airplane accidents, etc. Some of these disasters are mentioned below to highlight the likelihood that there may still be traces of them within the communities where they occurred; sociodramatists who work in these countries will probably feel the effects from them in the present.

The severity of an event is often assessed by the number of deaths caused by the disaster. According to this criterion, probably the most devastating natural disaster was the Black Death (or Great Plague), which killed about a third of Europe's population in the mid fourteenth century. In recent history, however, the deadliest disaster was probably the 2004 Indian Ocean earthquake that generated a tsunami that killed over 300,000 people.

Recent earthquakes in Peru (1970), Iran (1990, 2003), Armenia (1988), Taiwan (1999), Guatemala (1976), India (1993, 2001), Chile (1960), Turkey (1999), Japan (1995) and Pakistan (2005) also killed more than 10,000 people each. Extreme weather with great floods caused millions of deaths in China and Vietnam and great devastation in the US in 2005. As a comparison, the European heat wave of 2003 caused about 35,000 deaths.

A great number of people have also died as a result of contractible diseases, such as smallpox, the Spanish flu, and AIDS. In addition, large-scale famines in China, India, the Far East, and Africa have caused the starvation of millions of people.

Among smaller disasters, we can mention the hundreds of people who perished as a result of accidental fires. For example, in 1998, there was a discotheque fire in Gothenburg, Sweden, in which 63 people were killed and many injured, leaving a deep mark on the devastated community. Similar accidental deaths have occurred as a result of explosions in coalmines, ammunition dumps, gas installations, factories, etc. and in plane crashes. Recent examples are Pan Am Flight 103 at Lockerbie in 1988 and TWA Flight 800 in Long Island in 1996. It is easy for people in general to empathize with the victims of these disasters because so many people fly today. Maritime disasters have also caused the deaths of thousands of people. One of the most famous was the *RMS Titanic*, which sunk in 1912, resulting in the drowning of 1518 people. More recently, the *MS Estonia* caused the death of 852 people in the Baltic Sea. Space travel accidents may also be a blow to an entire nation, such as the space shuttle *Columbia* disaster in 2003.

While these natural and accidental events certainly were immense tragedies for the families of the victims, the greatest number of preventable deaths has been caused by deliberate acts of violence inflicted by human beings upon one another. We must shamefully acknowledge that many of the worst atrocities have occurred in our own time.

The Second World War was unquestionably the single most fatal man-made disaster. About 55 million people were killed in that terrible war between 1937 and 1945, including civilians who died from disease, famine, and atrocities; deaths of soldiers in battle; and the genocide of the Nazi Holocaust. The second deadliest event was probably the Cultural Revolution in China in which about 40 million died during Mao Zedong's regime (1949–1976), including the famine of that time. The third was the atrocities inflicted by the communist regime of the Soviet Union under Stalin from 1924 to 1953, in which about 20 million people perished (including the famine in the Ukraine). In comparison, about 15 million people were killed during the entire First World War and about 3 million people during the Vietnam War (1945–1975).

After all these wars, the yearning for peace has never been greater. However, the violence continues everywhere as if the human species has learned nothing from the past. Even after January 12 1951, when the Genocide Convention came into force, there have been many new genocides, such as the one in East Bengal (East Pakistan, 1971), the selective genocide of Hutus in Burundi (1972), the killing fields and genocide of the Khmer Rouge in Cambodia (1975–1979), the genocide in the Maya Highlands in Guatemala (1981–1983), the Anfal Campaign in Kurdistan by Iraq (1987–1988), the Serbian ethnic cleansing of Bosnian Muslims in Bosnia-Herzegovina (1992–1995), and the Akazu Hutu Power genocide of Tutsis in Rwanda (1994).

In Africa, vivid memories of the terrible genocide of Tutsis and Hutus in Rwanda, as well as the wars in Uganda, Sudan, and other African countries, still haunt entire communities. The apartheid era is also fresh in the minds of citizens of South Africa, and the Chinese people are still upset about the lack of recognition within the Japanese education system of the atrocities inflicted during the Nanking Massacre in 1937. During that terrible event, the Japanese army engaged in a premeditated and systematic campaign of mass murder that left more than one-quarter million Chinese dead. Similarly, for millions of Armenians around the globe, the wounds of the Armenian Genocide between 1915 and 1923 remain open because the world has not faced up to the truth (Kalayjian *et al.* 1996).

In sum, according to the statistics of the Stockholm International Peace Research Institute (SIPRI), there are presently about 30 armed conflicts in progress, a number that has remained more or less constant since 1986. Unfortunately, new trauma occurs on a daily basis, with the same long-term consequences for survivors of the various conflicts.

The relatively new phenomenon of terrorism has also created tens of thousands of victims. The most lethal terrorist attacks ever carried out were the series of coordinated attacks in the US on September 11 2001, which resulted in a death toll of almost 3000. These attacks did not only create a collective trauma for the American nation but affected the entire world (Pyszczynski, Solomon and Greenberg 2003). A year after the attack, Ayoub (2002) observed how our world has changed:

> [T]he intellectual understanding that we so prize at this institution of higher learning would not remove from any of our minds the images of the planes colliding into the World Trade Center or the growing awareness of the enormity of September 11th. Our lives were changed.

Much of what we were feeling and thinking – the numbing calm followed by tears, the sense that time had stopped or changed directions, the floating, dislocated sensations – were adaptive and protective coping strategies that helped us "survive" as we struggled to find safety again.

For the American population, September 11 brought back memories of earlier disasters in the US during the twentieth century, such as the Great Depression, Pearl Harbor, McCarthyism, the Cuban Missile Crisis, the assassinations of John F. Kennedy and Martin Luther King, Jr., the Vietnam War, and Watergate. There are also other, more distant, major traumatic events in the history of the US that still influence American society and which recently have received more attention. The first is the depopulation of at least 2 million Native Americans after 1492 (Manson *et al.* 1996) and the second is the death of between 6 million and 60 million Africans in the transatlantic slave trade during the sixteenth and nineteenth centuries. According to Eyerman (2002), slavery became a cultural marker that still influences the consciousness of every African-American today. In addition to the US Civil War (1861–1865), these historic events have surely shaped the collective unconscious of the American people until today.

Terrorist attacks that target the civilian population have become a daily phenomenon. We regularly witness cruel bombings in airplanes, trains, embassies, hotels, and buses in Madrid, Istanbul, Bali, Israel, England, Ireland, and various other places. The effects of such events are not only the direct and immediate death toll and the many injured but also the more widespread terror that in itself is experienced by the population at large. For example, the attack on the Beslan School in Russia in 2004 brought widespread despair not only to the small community that lost so many of its children and youth but also to the entire population of Russia, which was severely shaken by the event.

Collective trauma, of course, is especially felt on memorial days when a country mourns its losses. On Memorial Day, May 2 2006, the state of Israel honored the 22,123 soldiers who had fallen in defense of the state and the 1358 victims of terrorist attacks. In addition, it commemorated the approximately 200 Jews who had been killed in terrorist or anti-Semitic attacks abroad since 1968. Terrorist attacks, suicide bombings, or shooting rampages in Israel target innocent civilians at home, on buses, on city streets, at weddings, in discos or pizzerias, in busy marketplaces or quiet neighborhoods. They may strike at any place and at any time. For Israelis, the fear and pain of terrorism have become part of daily life. Though people still move about as usual, the impact of the attacks is slowly taking its toll. Israelis seem to be constantly "living on the edge" and many worry that a new bomb will explode at any time. Many jump at every loud noise and there is a high level of interpersonal suspicion and violence on the street. The thousands of bereaved families of the victims – the mothers and fathers and brothers and sisters and children – struggle with their immense grief and suffer constant emotional pain. All this collective mourning has become part and parcel of what it means to be an Israeli (Dasberg *et al.* 1987).

In Latin America, the long history of military dictatorship, armed conflict, and oppression have also left a deep mark on the fabric of society in the various countries of that region. Finally, there are also tensions that remain in Europe between (and within) the various parts of the former Yugoslavia, Turkey, Greece, and the former USSR to mention just a few.

Collective responses to trauma

The word *trauma* was originally used as a surgical concept, indicating a breaking point of body tissue. It later became a useful metaphor for a psychological breaking point in the lives of people who experienced great misfortune outside the range of ordinary human experience.

The common responses of people unable to cope adequately with the stressful events were summarized within the diagnosis of post-traumatic stress disorder (PTSD). This condition consists of anxiety and depression, as well as various other signs of emotional turmoil and mental distress. The person continues to reexperience the trauma (in vivid recollections and nightmares), has reduced interest in the external world, and suffers from various more or less physical symptoms such as hyper-alertness and sleep disturbances (American Psychiatric Association 1994).

> Frequently, there is a contradictory effort both to remember and to forget what happened and both to approach and to avoid the traumatic event in a compulsive repeated fashion. Like a broken record that is spinning around and around, intrusive experienced images and painful memories keep coming back while there is a conscious effort to avoid them and not to think about them. Desperate and often futile efforts are attempted to regain some kind of inner balance and emotional equilibrium. (Kellermann 2000, p.24)

The individual perspective on traumatization guides most of the public intervention data collection process after wars and disasters (Erickson 1994). The

International Red Cross, for example, routinely gathers information about the effects of war on individuals, small groups, and families at the microlevel. However, there is almost no consideration of the effects of massive trauma on the society as a whole from a sociological, macrolevel perspective. In addition, while individual traumatization has been well documented in literature, collective trauma (de Young 1998) with its psychological effects on an entire society has hitherto been less studied.

This situation, however, is beginning to change; and there is today a wide range of political scientists and sociologists who have particularly targeted this field of research. For example, in his study on the impact on the Israeli public of the assassination of Prime Minister Yitzhak Rabin in 1995, Verzberger (1997) concluded that, despite the magnitude of the event and intensity of the immediate response, the effects were short-lived. His definition of collective political trauma was based on the earlier work of the American Psychiatric Association (1994, pp.424–425), Erikson (1994, p.230), Janoff-Bulman (1992, p.59), and Moore and Fine (1990, pp.199–200). According to Verzberger (1997):

> collective political trauma is a shattering, often violent event that affects a community of people (rather than a single person or a few members of it), and that results from human behavior that is politically motivated and has political consequences. Such an event injures in one sharp stab, penetrating all psychological defensive barriers of participants and observers, allowing no space for denial mechanisms and thus leaving those affected with an acute sense of vulnerability and fragility. (p.864)

Many similar studies have been published and there is presently more awareness than previously of the importance of also looking at collective and cultural (deVries 1996) responses to trauma. In fact, because much of the healing is expected to evolve from the community, it is important to focus on such collective responses when mapping human responses to disasters.

There are presently a number of international aid agencies providing immediate psychological support and counseling after major disasters, such as the UN International Strategy for Disaster Reduction (ISDR) and the Academy for Disaster Management Education Planning and Training (ADEPT). Only a few days after the recent Asia–Pacific tsunami, for instance, it became evident that physical trauma in the unsettled population was minimal while almost everyone was displaying symptoms of psychological trauma. As a result, ADEPT trained hundreds of local community counselors to provide community-level psychosocial support to the affected population.

In such a mapping of collective trauma, we try to find answers to several questions. How does this specific society respond to the stressful event? What makes the collective trauma more or less severe? What makes it easier or more difficult for the society to cope with the trauma? Which are the aggravating and mitigating circumstances?

In attempting to answer these questions, we realize that the severity of a trauma, or amount of emotional suffering that is experienced by the survivor population, is influenced by several different factors, summarized by the four Ps: (a) predictability and preparation, (b) preventability, (c) purpose, and (d) periodic duration.

First, a community that has already been hit by a specific trauma will often *prepare* itself for the possibility of it happening again and will try to mobilize its various resources to be ready for the next disaster. The second time it happens might therefore be less chaotic and surprising. Second, an event seems to be more traumatic if we believe that we could have *prevented* it from occurring had we seen the warning signs when there was still time. Some major maritime disasters are examples of such trauma that could have been prevented. These naturally evoke a great deal of anger in the families of the victims at the authorities who failed to prevent the disaster from happening. Based on this rationale, people are even more upset when the trauma is caused with intentional *purpose*. Genocides carried out deliberately by one group of people upon another exacerbate the traumatic responses. Finally, events can be categorized as more or less severe according to the *duration* of their exposure. Thus, events that occur only once during a very short time may be perceived as less painful than those that are cumulative or sequential (such as the continuing exposure to stress for a long time with periods of danger interrupted by periods of safety).

These mitigating and aggravating circumstances, however, are generally more complex than this. Verzberger (1997) observed:

> In attributing the event to avoidable causes, members of the affected community are better able to cope with the posttraumatic anxieties about loss of control and the possible repetition of similar traumatic events in the future; they feel that they deal with known risks and therefore are better positioned to control their environment and prevent any further disasters (Foa, Zinbarg and Rothbaum 1992; Verzberger 1990, pp.116–117). Such beliefs are not necessarily founded on realistic

assessments, but they induce hope and reduce the despair and apathy that would be generated by a sense of helplessness. The expectation of controllability provides an incentive for proactive preparations to prevent future events of the same type and for planfully coping with their consequences if they happen (Suedfeld 1997). (p.870)

Despite these preliminary observations, we are still only at the beginning of our understanding of the wide-ranging effects of trauma upon society. In addition, we must conclude that there can be no adequate comparison of various disasters in terms of the emotional pain that they arouse in the survivors. According to Bauer (2001):

> No gradation of human suffering is possible. A soldier who lost a leg and a lung at Verdun suffered. How can one measure his suffering against the horrors that Japanese civilians endured at Hiroshima? How can one measure the suffering of a Roma woman at Auschwitz, who saw her husband and children die in front of her eyes, against the suffering of a Jewish woman at the same camp who underwent the same experience? Extreme forms of human suffering are not comparable, and one should never say that one form of mass murder is "less terrible" or even "better" than another. (p.13)

What we do know, however, is that there are some common phases of collective responses to major disasters that most communities pass through and that these seem to be fairly universal across different cultures.

Phases of collective trauma

Collective trauma follows a distinct course. In the history of a specific traumatic event, we can usually discern six phases of trauma responses:

1. onset of the actual event (the shock phase)

2. the time immediately after the event (the reactive phase)

3. a few weeks or months after the event (the coping phase)

4. many months, or years, after the event (the long-term effect)

5. generations after the event (the transgenerational transmission of trauma)

6. centuries after the event (the universal influence of trauma on the history of humankind).

These phases are very similar to the ones described in individuals who go through the process of crises or mourning, even though they occur to the group as a whole.

During the first phase of the traumatic event, sometimes called the shock phase, there is chaos and disorder and an inability to perceive fully and comprehend what is happening. This is the time for first responders to practice their skills: the police, firefighters, medical emergency teams, and military personnel, if needed. Usually employed by the government, these first responders indicate the level of preparedness of the society for a catastrophe and will inevitably also reflect the functioning of its political leadership.

A community that is exposed to a very stressful event is overwhelmed and in a state of emotional and cognitive turmoil. In this acute state, people experience either numbness and disbelief or hysteria and a breakdown of mental energy. For example, during a terrorist bombing, there is widespread confusion until the emergency personnel have arrived at the scene and correctly appraised the event. In more protracted disastrous events, such as those that occur during war, the psychological responses will often be put aside until more life-threatening concerns have been addressed.

Because confusion and a lack of knowledge tend to aggravate public anxieties, the role of the media to get the information out to the general public quickly cannot be overestimated. Such correct and "balanced" media coverage has been known to shorten significantly this first phase of shock. During this critical first phase, adequate *and sensitive* media coverage may therefore significantly influence the various public responses to the stressful event. For example, because transmitting horrifying images of the effects of terrorist attacks to mass audiences would create mass hysteria and serve the terrorists' interest, most TV stations today minimize direct exposure of gruesome and frightening pictures as much as possible so as not to traumatize the public vicariously. If utilized correctly, television can even contribute to the collective healing of the public, as pointed out by Stossel (2001):

> What is normally one of television's great weaknesses – its tendency toward manipulative sentimental exploitation – may prove to be an aid toward recovering from this national trauma. In many cases, as after the *Challenger* explosion and the Oklahoma City bombing, the media pries voyeuristically into the private reactions of victims' families, seeking mawkish drama on the cheap. But in the week after the [September 11] attacks, my initial revulsion at what looked to be yet another instance of emotional pornography gave way to the recognition that, in this

instance, perhaps uniquely, the heart-wrenching stories of people looking (in vain, alas) for their missing loved ones in Lower-Manhattan hospitals were actually providing a useful social function. As painful as these segments are to watch, and as uncomfortable as it makes me to see TV reporters serving as psychoanalysts and grief counselors (many of them sincerely overcome with emotion themselves), broadcasting these stories does seem to be helping the victims' families to deal with the loss of hope and to begin to grieve. Hearing these stories also helps lend a flesh-and-blood reality to a tragedy otherwise so unfathomably horrible as to be merely abstract. (p.35)

In the second, reactive, phase of the immediate aftermath of the event, people start to become aware of what has happened, try to assess the damage done, and begin to respond emotionally to the loss and destruction. They realize that they have survived and must now start to cope with the disastrous effects of the event. Groups of people might spontaneously join together to express their feelings of protest, fear, and rage towards the object that caused the disaster or towards their own leadership who were unable to protect them sufficiently. Collective responses can be emotional (fear that it will happen again), cognitive (inability to understand what happened), interpersonal (a wish to be together or alone), and behavioral (avoidance of anything that reminds them of the disastrous event).

During this phase, it is important simply to sit and talk with the survivors, listen to them, and be a part of their loss. For instance, after the tsunami, survivors needed someone from their own community to empathize with them; community counselors provided support by helping the bereaved express their grief, handling the children through play, and organizing interactive and creative activities, such as enacting plays, composing poems, singing songs, dancing and music, etc., with the themes of "goodness of nature," "tsunami is transient," "we shall overcome," etc. In addition, they provided public education and awareness of the nature of the tsunami and specific problem-solving and supportive activities.

The immediate period following a traumatic event is a crucial time in the process of recovery. During this time, a narrative of the trauma is generated and constructed alongside a process of cognitive processing of the traumatic events.

All of these factors influence the coping ability of the affected population. A resilient society will be able to take a step back to address the problem, seek help from others, and motivate its members to get involved in the community and help one another. During this stage, it is wise to enlist various resource persons who demonstrate a sense of mastery. Because of their earlier experiences of coping with many different crises, such persons will be able to encourage a positive and proactive outlook and help develop social support networks to care for the more vulnerable populations within the society.

Naturally, any catastrophic event will affect the national mood and coherent national identity of a country. As a result and because trauma shakes the very basic structure of social cohesion, there will be both centripetal and centrifugal effects at work that bring people together and move them apart. There can be a voice expressing the feeling that "We stand united against a common enemy!" and another voice that emphasizes protest and blame for the deleterious events that happened. Various types of leaders – political and religious – will sometimes utilize both powerful social processes for their own purposes.

According to Volkan (2001), there is a kind of societal regression at this stage that is intrinsically neither good nor bad but an inevitable and necessary response to such trauma. As illustrated by the events following September 11, the main task for the group and its leader during this time is to maintain, protect, modify, or repair their shared group identity.

In the third phase of trauma (coping or breaking), which sets in a few weeks or months after the event and often continues for many years, the outcome is often unpredictable. Because there is a great difference in the ability of different communities to deal adequately with the stressful event, this phase is characterized by a great deal of soul searching. Delayed responses put further pressure on the society and there is a kind of "testing of the limits" for how much each society can take before it breaks apart.

The social structure of each community will only be able to cope with a certain amount of stress. While many societies may be able to work through their loss and readjust to the new reality, others will remain stuck in a state of disorganization as a result of their inability to integrate the painful experiences adequately. If there is more social support and social cohesiveness, such as during times of war against a common enemy, there seem to be fewer psychiatric breakdowns, suicides, and manifestations of collective trauma.

At one time or another, however, there will be a question of when a community should move on or remain stuck in the processing of the event. Moving on will mean trying to forget about the event, to avoid dealing with its painful consequences, and, if the society cannot face up to the realities, to deny that the event ever happened in the first place.

In the process of working through the trauma, most societies have a tendency during this phase to shun the actual victims of trauma, the war veterans and the torture victims and the survivors of genocide. It is cruel that people who have stood face to face with the Angel of Death and have paid a high personal price for the society will often be treated as social outcasts by many societies during this time. They are not only avoided, but even hidden and rejected and told to keep their experiences to themselves because they carry a message of shame and vulnerability that is highly disturbing for many. It seems to be a universal (but unfair) phenomenon that a society wants to push memories of the trauma out of its consciousness (and memory) during this time of reorganization (Gray and Oliver 2004). As a result of such collective repression, there is an illusory sense of gradual distance-building from the traumatic event and people act as if nothing had happened. Instead, they are occupied with practical matters, such as rebuilding what was destroyed and recreating the families that were killed.

Leaders of the communist USSR regime were world champions in erasing awkward past history from public view. Being notoriously known for playing with the facts of history, they erased names and faces at the mere whim of a czarist henchman or communist party member. The ruling power simply deleted from their history books facts, happenings, and names that they did not want people to know. For example, Khrushchev denounced and deleted Stalin; Breznev overthrew and deleted Khrushchev; and Gorbachev, who began the liberal changes that ultimately brought about the collapse of the Soviet Union in 1991, deleted Breznev.

While there can be some short-term positive effects of such burial of tragic history, the backside of this collective repression is that it prevents a society from preparing itself for similar future events and from learning from the past. As a result, each second or third generation seems to be forced to make the same mistakes as the earlier one, without any cumulative collective learning process ever happening.

In the fourth phase of trauma, which commences after five or ten years and may continue for half a decade or longer, the long-term effects gradually or suddenly reappear within individuals and communities. After an apparent silent period, when memories of the trauma have been buried or "put into storage," they will suddenly erupt with force. Sometimes, they will come out as the result of a trigger event, such as a new trauma that reminds people of the old one that had not been sufficiently resolved. At other times, the general *Zeitgeist* ("the spirit of the time") may have become ripe for starting to deal with the historic event in a more unemotional manner. The Holocaust as a collective trauma of the Jewish people is a good illustration of this gradual process of uncovering, even though it happened over 60 years ago.

In the fifth phase of collective trauma, signs will appear of transgenerational transmission of trauma to the children of the survivors.

In his paper on the intergenerational aspects of the conflict in the former Yugoslavia, Klain (1998) described the transmission of hate and rage, revenge and guilt, through "mediators" such as the family, the superego, folk songs, literature, myths, the church, and religion. In such secondary collective trauma, the effects are obviously fundamentally different from the effects of the primary traumatization. It is not the catastrophic event in itself that is the crucial factor but a long-term socialization process in which the traumatic "content" has become implanted into the conscious and unconscious minds of the offspring (Kellermann 2001b).

Like infectious disease, collective trauma can be thus transmitted from parent to child or from a majority of the community to all its members. Schützenberger (2000) described how such transmission may occur from generation to generation through the various "invisible loyalties" (Boszormenyi-Nagy and Spark 1973) that are constructed within families. Utilizing genosociograms and psychodramatic enactments to put light on the individual's emotional family heritage, she showed how an "anniversary syndrome" (a kind of family curse) can reappear at a significant date many generations after the original trauma.

Finally, in the sixth phase of trauma, we can sometimes observe the universal effects of the catastrophic event. Such generalized effects are inflicted on humankind in general or on a specific ethnic group or national entity in particular, remaining forever a part of its essential cultural marker. Such signs include general cultural stereotypes that become an inherent part of the collective beliefs. They are also a part of the myths, traditions, and sagas of all civilization. As collective memory finds its way into oral history, the traumatic events are told and retold by the elderly and become part of the culture, carried forward across generations in the literature, law, and the structure of society.

In an extraordinary paper on the transgenerational memory of culture and society, Perry (1999) observed that the memory of a trauma is carried not only through family myths, childrearing practices, and belief systems but also in the neurobiology of the individual. It is the unique property of living systems to carry forward such elements of the past. A collective memory becomes in a very true sense a dynamic system that carries its own history forward in time through the apparatus of neurobiological mechanisms related to the collective memory passed from generation to generation over the centuries.

From this perspective, we may look at the collective consciousness of human beings as being a large compilation of tragic events and disasters – a cumulative mass of trauma for thousands of years. While most of these have perhaps been relegated to the dark abyss of the unconscious, they continue to have some impact and they also make themselves heard from time to time. As I explained in the beginning of this chapter, remnants of such old traumatic events remain as sediment within the inner lives of human beings. Like deposits in our blood, sediments of traumatic past experiences follow us everywhere. It is as if something is stored away for safekeeping – a repository of ancient tragedy – not unlike the significant artifacts and memorabilia stored away in a museum, a book, or a burial place.

Collective trauma will always remain a very elusive phenomenon that is confined largely within the unconscious sphere. As a result, any collective trauma will sooner or later become part of the "collective unconscious," something that is discussed further in chapter 3.

For most survivors of collective trauma, the terrible events will not be incorporated and stored as a regular part of their memories or remain a part of their ordinary personal histories to be told to subsequent generations. The tragedy will remain as a part of the more or less fragmented parts of themselves and as something that has interrupted the normal flow of their life histories. Sociodrama tries to liberate them from the history of collective trauma and from the hidden agendas it has imposed.

Some sociodrama sessions may recreate a whole history of past tragedies in a single session. For example, in a recent sociodrama workshop in the Ukraine, the group started with a reenactment of the social upheaval ("Orange Revolution") and the election of Victor Yushchenko. As the session proceeded, however, and we were searching for traces of earlier sociopolitical underpinnings, other events surfaced. The most obvious was relations with the Soviet Union and the 72 years of communism during which people suffered severe political persecution. In addition, the group expressed the pain of the Holodomor famine in which over 10 million Ukrainians starved to death. (This famine occurred before the Second World War trauma and the occupation by Nazi Germany.) Thus, the after-effects of all of these collective traumatic events were actualized within a single sociodrama session in 2005.

3

Societry

The earlier two chapters have discussed how sociodrama can be used to help groups explore and work through their emotional responses to collective trauma. In the present chapter, I will put this approach within a larger frame of reference and delineate some of the other applications of sociodrama that will be discussed throughout this book.

In common with many early sociologists, Moreno (1953) conceived society as an organism that can be either sick or healthy. A sick society would be cured with "societry," which was a paraphrase of psychiatry: the treatment of individual mental illness. Sociatrists within the social sciences would be the counterparts of psychiatrists within psychiatry and a group of individuals would be "sociotic" rather than psychotic (Moreno 1953, p.379). Instead of utilizing common mental health cures, sociatrists would use "sociatric" methods, such as socioanalysis (Haskell 1962), clinical sociology, group psychotherapy, and especially sociodrama.

Such a biological analogy to society is obsolete today and terms such as "socio-pathology" (Lemert 1951) have been largely replaced by terms such as social "disintegration," a term which is not based on an organic model of society. For heuristic purposes, however, we will maintain this medical analogy to look at some social ailments that could be "treated" by different applications of sociodrama.

But what is a "sick society"? Is it a society with pain? With conflict? With some kind of imbalance? What are the intragroup and intergroup criteria that we should apply to such a medical model of sociopathology? When we have defined such a state of "sociopathology," how do we start to heal it? And when does a society become "normal"?

In order to answer these questions, this chapter will attempt to provide a general theory of sociopathology based on the detrimental effects of collective trauma upon a society. After a brief discussion of the basic idea of a society as a patient and the group as a "we," I will define some relevant concepts pertaining to this general theory, such as "collective consciousness" and "chosen trauma." This will enable us to conceptualize how members of a society who are overwhelmed by a stressful event develop sociopathology by tending to cluster together within their common identity while forming a collectively repressed unconscious shadow of their past, tragic history. This shadow will, in turn, continue to haunt them for generations, demanding a psychosocial treatment approach such as sociodrama.

Society as a patient

A society seen as an ailing person first must undergo some kind of assessment or diagnosis. Any such mental health evaluation of a society would include an assessment of the history, age, geography, and general description of the society to be followed by more in-depth analysis of its internal and external relations, its dreams and fantasies (or cultural heritage and folklore), and, finally, its chief complaint and symptomatology. From our present perspective of collective trauma, we would naturally pay extra attention to major disasters in its recent or past history and try to connect these with the present complaints.

Various kinds of sociopathology may be initially described in terms of classical social complaints, such as crime, ethnic strife, unemployment, addiction, poverty, global warming, or political chaos. In addition, social ailments use the theory and language of psychiatry and apply them to describe social phenomena. This latter terminology diagnoses social phenomena in a way similar to individual psychiatric nosology but would in this framework be expressed as social psychopathology. Terms such as public stress, collective paranoia, group anxiety, or mass psychosis can be used in these cases. After all, such descriptive psychosocial terms are abundant not only in the popular literature but also in the professional social science literature. For instance, Williams (2001) suggested a graph-like system to monitor the *psychological climate* of any society for consideration by politicians in their decision-making process after major political changes, conflicts, or disasters.

The self-image of a society can also be diagnosed. For instance, if encountering an ethnic group with strong cohesion and pride in its own cultural heritage, we can describe it as overly narcissistic or ethnocentric. All this material creates a sociopolitical profile with its own theory and its own practice that assists sociodramatists in their initial assessments and provides the rationale for the suggested methods and strategies.

Naturally, any attempt to study a society as a group as a whole and in real life immediately confronts us with a tremendous number of perspectives and details. Trying to get an overall picture of what is happening in a society is a formidable undertaking, including amassing information on government, schools, hospitals, employment, prisons, public communications, mass media, religious institutions, neighborhoods, emergency services, etc. The fact that everything changes constantly is an additional problem. Attempting to describe and understand all of these elements and their interrelations is an impossible task. Difficult choices must, therefore, be made as to what to look at when attempting such an appraisal.

These choices should not be made in an arbitrary fashion but should be guided by the primary purpose of our work. Depending on what we are interested in knowing about the society, it is sufficient, in some circumstances, to know only a few things, such as the economic situation and demographics of a society. In another, we have to dig deep into the very structure of that society and try to discover the hidden but distinctive patterns in its past history and modern development. If we look at the problem of child abuse, for example, we may discover a specific group culture with its own distinctive values, morals, and ways of childrearing prevalent in that society. Or, if looking at national identity, we may try to define the "true self" of that specific society, the essence of being a member of this community with all its cultural and religious ramifications.

Some societies are more self-aware and scrutinizing while others are fully unaware or unconscious of their own goals and motives. If a society is dominated by a strong religious faith, we can expect a social system of self-control or superego structure that usually has a profound influence on its people. Similarly, the pervasive customs and traditions of a specific society will determine much of their members' social behavior. This behavior will provide us with a sense of the general atmosphere of that society and give us a feeling for the society as a more or less nurturing environment for human beings to live in. We would ask questions like: Is it a good or bad place for children to grow up in? Is it enabling or restrictive? Is it accommodating of minorities and those who are not like everybody else?

Answering these questions within a sociatric assessment would end with a description of the specific social structure that has been observed, including what a society expects certain people to do to fit in, how flexible it is, and how social and public services are provided. A description of such phenomena may use terms such as status and role, role conflicts, social classes, social groups, etc.

and give some clues as to where our interventions may have the most initial impact.

Moreno was deeply engaged in how to conduct such a general appraisal of a society. His various sociometric and group research projects were constructed to study a multitude of social processes and forces that were more or less healthy for the population at large.

"We"

A major problem in any such assessment is delineating the society that we want to evaluate. Who is the patient group? And who are the "we" that we talk about when we describe ourselves as belonging to that specific group? What are its commonalities and what are the characteristics of this assemblage of persons who are gathered or located together?

When investigating a society or something collective, we sometimes refer to a small or large group, a nuclear family or the entire clan, a tribe, a class in school or the entire school, a staff team at work or the entire workplace, a community or an entire township, a country or a union of countries, or the entire species of human beings on earth. All these are collective entities that can be looked upon as societies that have some common characteristics and can experience collective trauma.

For Moreno, the group in sociodrama refers to a larger social unit than the small group. Therefore, sociodrama can be conducted at the level of microsociology, exploring details of particular interactions as they manifest themselves in everyday life, or at the level of macrosociology, focusing on the broader structure of large organizations, such as those comprising cities, states, and entire countries. When describing the social system of societies at any of these levels, sociodramatists apply concepts of individual dynamics to the group as if it could behave, feel, and think like an individual.

Sociologists have described how entire communities come together in solidarity for various common purposes and how they feel knit together in tight fellowship. Much of this commonality is based on the fact that they share a collective worldview.

Every time we say the word "we," we refer to that which is common to us all. At such moments, we combine a group of people into a generalized whole. But when we talk "for" the group, it is as if we talk about one person only – as if the group had a single motivational force, so to speak. Like in the creation of a salad made from different ingredients, there is an extra dimension added to the collected mixture, which is essentially different from its separate compo-nents. It is this "surplus value" that is the central element of the group. This central element is the common denominator among the people in general and best characterizes the collective elements in this group. For example, it includes all that is characteristic and meaningful in what we call "The British." It is the sense of belonging and recognition that British soldiers feel when going to war and being willing to die for their country. It is part of their cultural or collective group identity, which Volkan and Itzkowitz (1994, p.11) likened to a large tent that protects the individuals "like a mother."

Naturally, the same thing is true for the Japanese, the Americans, Norwegian fishermen, or any group that feels some pride of belonging to "their own people." It is also true for any countrymen and women who are proud when "their own" team wins a medal at the Olympic Games. Hundreds and thousands of years of tribal mentality have molded people into such well-defined cultural entities.

Clearly, these cluster tendencies are reinforced in times of major disasters or threats by another tribe, such as in war. These tendencies not only forge a group's national cohesiveness and their sense of "we" but also empower people to cope with the outer threat. In fact, the group that has jointly endured a collective trauma will almost automatically form a common base of mutual affinity with a high degree of cohesion, often described in terms of "we who have endured this or that terrible experience…"

Chosen trauma

When an ethnic group uses the memory of a victorious or a disastrous event for specific purposes, the political psychoanalyst Volkan (1991, 1992, 1997, 2004) called it a "chosen glory" or a "chosen trauma." Such a significant event becomes a mythological identity marker for the large group; it brings group members together and provides the group with a common history that can be retold from generation to generation. As years go by, the large group becomes identified with the event and its accompanying emotions, defenses, fantasies, and mythologies. According to Volkan, a "chosen trauma" with its characteris-tic sense of victimization, humiliation, failure to mourn, and massive repres-sion of fear and anxiety, as well as primitive good/bad splitting processes, provides a justification for having enemies and for taking violent revenge. Because of unresolved collective trauma, there is, according to Volkan, a recurring cycle of violence between ethnic groups who will fight one another for generations.

From my experience with Holocaust survivors, I find that such an analysis and its main concepts are largely inadequate for explaining how past collective trauma influences the present behavior of large groups. First, a traumatized group of people rarely chooses to identify with the victim role. Most of them view themselves as survivors who have succeeded in coping and have maintained their human qualities despite everything. They detest utilizing their suffering for public purposes and vehemently protest when others do so. In addition, during my study trip to the countries of the former Yugoslavia in 2006, I was unable to verify Volkan's (1997) interpretation of the Serbian chosen trauma from his book *Bloodlines*.

Second, the term *chosen trauma* is inherently obscure and rather misleading. It indicates that someone has purposefully chosen to become violated, abused, or oppressed; and, as such, it is not only doubtful but also unfair and offensive. While Volkan clearly stated that a group does not choose to be victimized, the term can easily be misunderstood as assigning responsibility for an injustice inflicted upon innocent victims. Because there is so much misunderstanding concerning the feelings of responsibility of any trauma survivor and because the tendency to adopt survival guilt in this population is so widespread, it is detrimental even to hint at something the victims have done to perpetuate their own suffering. In addition, to indicate that a group has "chosen" a mental representation (even if it is done unconsciously) seems to be unfair under the circumstances. It is my view that the concept of "invisible loyalties" (Boszormenyi-Nagy and Spark 1973), while referring to the system of families and not to large groups, may be much more suitable as a description of these transgenerational transmission processes than Volkan's concept of chosen trauma.

Finally, the simple correlation of past suffering with the present inclination for violence and revenge is largely hypothetical. While it is certainly possible and plausible that some ethnic groups want to take revenge against a group that had earlier inflicted harm on them and that this first group inflicts violence in the name of their chosen trauma, there are so many other variables influencing group violence that this purpose seems of minor significance.

I make these critical comments also in response to Volkan's (2004) suggestion that Israelis have been utilizing the Holocaust as a chosen trauma, or as a collective identity marker, to justify their aggression toward Palestinians and that the support for hard-line politics in Israel is generated by the suppression of grief, shame, and fear stemming from the Holocaust. This theory was later reiterated by Scheff (2004) to explain the public support for Sharon's destructive policies toward the Palestinians as an expression of their chosen trauma and their suppression of grief, shame, and fear. The theory simply assumes that people go to war not because of a desire to conquer or because of any evil instinct but because they (unconsciously) want to act out an old (chosen) trauma. Since this chosen trauma led to humiliating defeat and the population was unable to mourn their losses, they became compelled to take revenge at a later time in history. As a result, anger was displaced and expressed against another enemy in a collective process of regression, splitting good ("we") and bad ("them") and glorifying a strong and omnipotent leader who is followed blindly.

My experience does not corroborate such an analysis. In fact, the opposite may be true. Many survivor groups, including Holocaust survivors, have a deep knowledge of the terrible consequences of violence, war, and oppression and are the first to adopt the nonviolence credo in intergroup conflicts, if at all possible. The assumption that former victims of violence later become perpetrators themselves cannot be substantiated at this time. While the Holocaust is certainly a collective trauma for the people of Israel and memories of past injustices naturally lead people to anticipate future oppression or violence, it does not automatically follow that the Holocaust is a chosen trauma utilized to justify military actions against the Palestinian population. It cannot be compared to the reasons suggested for the war in the former Yugoslavia. In fact, this theory neglects to observe an exactly opposite phenomenon in which a left-wing Israeli population is more than willing to make compromises because of its earlier experiences and despite all the present threats.

The theories of Volkan and Scheff about the existence of an unfinished old trauma behind all collective violence represent the kind of popular but distorted thinking that seems to dominate many social scientists in our time. The only problem with these theories is that they are blind to any possible real threat from "evil" forces that seek nothing less than to cause death and destruction (see chapter 7). That emotions underlie aggressive behavior goes without saying. To generalize all violence to unconscious processes, however, is a little bit too much to swallow. Naturally, there are many more reasons to go to war, including the very basic instinct of people to defend themselves from outside threats. No narrow view will help us understand the roots of collective violence, neither can they be the only basis of our sociodramatic work;

collective mourning and other social rituals will by themselves be insufficient to guide us towards any real peace in the world.

My critique of Volkan's concept of chosen trauma, however, does not include the basic assumption that any significant event, and particularly a collective trauma, becomes a mythological identity marker for the large group. This, I believe, is a universal phenomenon. In addition, I have repeatedly observed how the group as a whole tries to repress any tragic memories and to treat them as taboo subjects. As such, they sooner or later become part of the collective secrets and unspoken memories of the community, relegated to the dark abyss of the collective unconscious of the society.

Collective unconscious

The French social theorist Émile Durkheim (1858–1917) coined the term *collective consciousness* to describe how a community shares similar values and how individuals are constrained by social forces embodied in the formal and informal norms and values of their culture. These are expressed in a variety of ways, ranging from codified rules and laws to more informal rules that exist only in the minds of the people who share those collective norms. While not always verbalized, these shared norms provide common ideological ground for members of a society and ensure that members act in agreed-upon ways.

Social psychology has contributed much to our understanding of how such social forces influence the group as a whole. These social forces have been variously called the "collective unconscious" (Jung 1953), "social unconscious" (Fromm 1962), "group mind" (McDougall 1920), "groupthink" (Janis 1972), "group pressure" and "group dynamics" (Lewin 1948), "basic assumption cultures" and "group mentality" (Bion 1961), "sociometry" and "co-unconscious" of the group (Moreno 1953), "group matrix" (Foulkes 1964), "common group tension" (Ezriel 1973), "invisible group" (Agazarian and Peters 1981), and "group focal conflict" (Whitaker and Lieberman 1964). All these terms depict the group as something more than the sum of its members, having its own (often concealed) goals, norms of behavior, patterns of communication, and power structure, which may produce social constraints and interpersonal conflicts. Morris (1969) provided one of the more colorful descriptions of people who build tribes in such a "human zoo."

In his book on the social unconscious, Hopper (2002) gave an in-depth analysis and discussion of how groups and their participants are constrained unconsciously by social, cultural, and political forces. Moreno suggested that, when the unconscious minds of several individuals are interlocked, it creates a kind of "co-unconscious" (Zuretti 1994), or collective unconscious, that provides a deep bond between these individuals. Moreno's emphasis was not on the collective (repressed) images of a given culture or of mankind but on the specific relatedness and cohesiveness of a group of individuals on the unconscious level. They feel affiliated to one another almost as if they belong to the same family.

Any small group is seen as a reflection of the society at large. By revealing some of the secrets of its collective group mind as reflected in the matrix (Foulkes 1964; Powell 1989, 1994) of the group as a whole (Schermer and Pines 1994), the sociodramatist may make some of these unconscious social processes more visible. When traumatic experiences are manifested in the unconscious life of groups, they are part of what Hopper (2003) called the "fourth basic assumption group." However, in contrast to group analysis, which is based only on verbal interpretation, sociodrama tries to translate these tacit processes into overt action.

There are various other terms used to characterize such public repression. According to Fromm (1962), the social unconscious of each society is composed of those thoughts and feelings that a society will not permit its members to harbor in awareness. There is a kind of social filtering process that forces these taboo conceptions of reality out of awareness because they are too painful for the group to acknowledge. Describing some of these same processes, Jung (1953) called them a part of the collective unconscious, the inherited and universal part of the unconscious identical in all people. This layer is revealed in archetypal symbols (represented within dreams, myths, fairy tales, and religion), which are mental images that help us recognize and integrate the parts of ourselves we have disowned or are apprehensive about. Fromm's concept of the social unconscious differed from the traditional Jungian concept of the collective unconscious with its emphasis on the inheritance of acquired characteristics. However, it is similar to Jungian views of the shared unconscious, emphasizing the interpersonal, the intersubjective, and socialization in general.

The collective unconscious reverberates deep in our souls and in the fabric of our being. It is the repository of our ontogenetic and phylogenetic heritage (including both our biological origin and development and our racial evolution). Similar to individual painful memories, which are repressed when they become overwhelming, collective memories of a disaster are pushed down into the abyss of the collective unconscious when they become unbearable and unacceptable for the community in which they occurred. Until there is sufficient strength to cope with them, they will be manifested only indirectly through interpolation and transformation, such as in the interpretation of cultural traditions and political ideologies and in the behavior of the public.

Example: sociodrama on asylum seekers

During the last few years, I have participated in several group sessions in Europe dealing with the problem of asylum seekers and with the consequences of the increasing diversity in many countries. The following is an amalgamated description of a sociodrama session that focused on this situation.

One of the group members worked as a teacher in a school of foreigners; she complained that almost all her students were immigrants. Another group member told the group that she also worked with immigrants who were uncertain that they could remain in the country. After a short discussion, the group decided to look at the general problem of immigrants and asylum seekers, and the director suggested that the group present the situation in action.

First, the urgent situation of Edna, the asylum seeker, was presented. The teacher explained that Edna was currently in the hospital; she had attempted suicide and remained in a very precarious state of mind. Edna was sure she would face further racism and physical abuse if deported to Kosovo, where she would be a burden to her seriously ill mother.

Many different people tried the role of Edna, the asylum seeker. One person said:

> I am in a bad state emotionally. Most nights I lie in bed feeling nervous, wondering about what will happen to me. I have not heard anything for a long time about my court case and feel that I could be deported any day. I do not think that I can stand this uncertainty any longer…

Another participant said:

> I would prefer to stay in this country, but it has taken so long to get a response from the immigration department. I have lost heart. I don't want to go back to Kosovo because of what happened to me there and because of my mother…I have been in hospital for so long now and I do not know what is happening…

She looked around to see if anyone was listening. Most participants seemed to empathize with Edna.

It was now the task of the group to take the lead in developing the story. The director was careful not to take over the problem-solving activity at this stage but rather handed it over to the group. As a result, other roles were introduced that had a direct impact on Edna's situation. For example, there were other asylum seekers who tried to provide support but who were also waiting for permission to stay in the country. Then, there were the friendly social workers, teachers, and nurses who also tried their best to be of assistance and who voiced their concern for Edna's well-being. They felt resentment at the community for not letting her stay. Finally, there were the various community representatives who clarified the rules and regulations of the country: the immigration workers, the police, and the government officials.

At this stage of the session, the group had presented the individual person (as a representative of a group of people), the immediate organization (which took the decision of what to do), and the larger society (that had made the policy decisions). The director presented each of the roles through a short interview: "Who are you? What do you think and feel? What do you want to say?" Each new role was thus introduced in turn: (a) the asylum seeker; (b) the social worker, the headmaster, the immigration official; and (c) the interior minister or prime minister. The director asked, "What do they all want? And how does this affect the asylum seeker and the society at large?"

To answer this question, a few classic situations were chosen in which some of these predicaments were played out. In rapid succession, the vignettes were presented, and with each new situation the problem was further clarified. But it also became more complicated. Personal emotions were constantly mixed with general concerns. The director utilized several techniques to describe and elaborate the situation as fully as possible and to let as many participants as possible experience the significant roles in the sociodrama. Thus, he suggested a role reversal between different asylum seekers, between the asylum seeker and the government representative, etc. He also asked someone to double one of the roles and express what that person was thinking and feeling but was unable to say aloud. As the drama unfolded as if by itself, participants gradually became more emotionally involved.

For example, in the middle of the conversation between Edna and a social worker, one spectator rose to voice the concerns of Edna's mother in Kosovo. The mother asked Edna to come home: "Things have become safe now and there is nothing to be afraid of here any longer!" Then, there was a moment of silence. Participants digested this new information, which was received with some surprise. The person who originally played Edna was again asked if she would like to stay or to return home. She hesitated.

Framing the situation as a choice of staying abroad or coming home, as opposed to being permitted to remain or being sent away, made a big difference. In addition, from the various comments of group members in the roles of government officials, it suddenly became clear that the issue had gone beyond the individual case of Edna and the immigration policy of a specific country. It now touched the very basis of pluralism in the entire Western world.

To elucidate the various opinions and positions on this issue, the director suggested introducing a few "politicians" to voice the various prevalent opinions. He asked, "Who is for 'people like Edna' staying in this country?" A few persons volunteered to represent a parliamentary committee on the issue. After a short discussion, they concluded that anyone coming must apply for a visa before they enter the country and that only those who are entitled to asylum should then be allowed to come. Some felt the asylum policy was too lenient and suggested removing thousands of asylum seekers who they felt had no right to stay in the country. Other members voiced the opposite opinion: "These people are refugees! Have some compassion. They have no other place to go; they would be in danger if they returned to their own country. Let them stay!"

The director asked them all to make their positions more extreme. One person said, "I am sick of the politicians and do-gooders saying they are welcome here. They are not! Those foreigners who came before respected our laws and customs, but these parasites who come now are only criminals!"

Another person, taking the role of a racist, added:

Yes, this is not a Muslim country. Let us look out for our own troubled people first, our own elderly, homeless, and poor. These people from Kosovo came with nothing and they gave us nothing. We should send them all back with nothing. We have become the dumping ground for Europe! We never wanted these people; we never asked them to come!

Apparently, participants were able to express the unspoken sentiments of the society in these roles. There was a sense of liberation and satisfaction at being able to say things that had hitherto been taboo.

As a result, emotions were high and the atmosphere tense. The drama had developed in its own direction. The director had only created a group norm in which free speech was allowed. As a result, there was also a freedom to enact different roles and to become personally involved. The process had been ignited with the magic of communication, and the doors had been opened both to conflict and to dialogue.

Two clear views were now presented: for or against asylum seekers, immigrants, and foreigners. Both sides voiced their positions in a convincing manner. At this point, the director stepped in and asked, "What could be a viable solution?" He asked the person who was against, "What are you afraid of? Why do you not want them to stay? Are you afraid that you will lose your national identity if he stays?" The person responded, "They can become a majority! And what will then become of us? Our white race will be annihilated!"

The other side was also asked questions and the person playing the more tolerant role shared with the group that he, himself, was the child of immigrants and felt that this country could benefit from new inhabitants because its birth rate was slowly decreasing.

The group then convened to discuss possible solutions. They suggested, for example, incorporating community relations work into preparations for asylum seekers' arrivals. For example, refugees and newcomers needed to be integrated into the society following their arrival and to participate in integrative activities, particularly for smaller groups who were dispersed widely. Finally, some participants suggested implementing antiracist training and awareness activities among the youth in schools and other places.

Various applications of sociodrama

Practitioners use sociodrama for various purposes. Some try to explore long-standing collective unconscious material repressed because of collective trauma. Others try to develop a deeper understanding of complex sociopolitical circumstances. Finally, others focus on intergroup conflicts to improve coexistence between groups that do not get along.

These different goals of sociodrama may be more or less categorized into five different applications of sociodrama. These applications of sociodrama, with their various focuses, theories, and ideals, are summarized in Table 3.1.

Table 3.1 Applications of sociodrama

Applications	Focus	Ideal
Crisis	Collective trauma	Safety
Political	Social disintegration	Equality
Diversity	Prejudice	Tolerance
Conflict management	Interpersonal tension	Peace
Postconflict reconciliation	Justice and rehabilitation	Coexistence

While all of these applications are closely interrelated (trauma leads to disintegration, which leads to prejudice, and then to renewed trauma), they are here separated for heuristic reasons. These applications will be further discussed in the chapters that follow: crisis sociodrama in chapter 4, political sociodrama in chapter 5, and diversity sociodrama in chapter 6. In addition, sociodramatic theory and the practice of conflict management will be presented in chapter 7. Finally, I will discuss intervention strategies for postconflict rehabilitation and reconciliation in chapter 8.

The first application, crisis sociodrama, deals with collective trauma and group responses to catastrophic events of national significance. The second application, political sociodrama, deals with social problems of power and equality. The third application, diversity sociodrama, deals with conflicts based on stereotypes, prejudice, racism, intolerance, stigmatization, or negative bias against people because of their diversity. The fourth application, sociodrama for conflict management, may set in motion individual and social processes that may transform violence into less dangerous ways of managing conflict. The final application of sociodrama deals with post-conflict reconciliation and community rehabilitation.

Sociodrama is sometimes criticized for being imbued with ethereal, pre-fabricated, utopian principles that may have philosophical validity applied to great masses of people but are too far divorced from the actual data of the individual unit of the mass to have practical utility. The goals of sociodrama may be rightly considered ambitious from a global perspective. Obviously, we do not have any simple solutions to the many social problems of the world. And, probably, there are no such simple solutions. But we must continue to search for solutions, believing that it will be easier to find them together than if each person tries to find them alone.

Naturally, permanent conflict abolition cannot be the final goal of sociodrama because tensions will continuously recur as long as people are together. Furthermore, to achieve social homeostasis as a result of crisis sociodrama, social equality as a result of political sociodrama, or social tolerance as a result of diversity sociodrama is imaginary, to say the least. Despite well-conducted and powerful sociodrama sessions, social traumatization, disintegration, and prejudice will surely continue to have detrimental influences on society. In addition, other strategies of peace promotion, such as direct negotiations between the disputants, preventive diplomacy, third party mediation, arbitration, and various peaceful settlements of disputes (Boutros-Ghali 1992), are surely more applicable to international conflict resolution (Burton 1986) than sociodrama.

Consequently, rather than formulating the goal of sociodrama in such exaggerated terms as human survival (Moreno 1953) or world peace, sociodrama should be more realistically appreciated as one of many activities that may help prepare for conflict resolution (Kaufman 1996; Rothman 1992). As such, it may have a unique potential for helping large groups of people work through their collective trauma so that, when the time is ripe, they may approach the struggles of human coexistence with more awareness. At such times, sociodrama may have a unique potential for bringing large groups of hostile people together and opening up new channels of communications between them. This includes the "bottom-up" approach to conflict resolution that should occur prior to diplomatic negotiations between enemies who have been involved in intergroup clashes. An example of this approach is the role played by John Alderdice, psychotherapist and leader of the Alliance Party, in relation to the beginning of peace negotiations in Northern Ireland.

Sociodrama may thus be seen as filling different functions in the various stages of the development and resolution of conflict. The first three kinds of sociodrama (crisis, politics, and diversity) may be viewed as dealing with preconflict issues and as preventive in nature. The fourth kind of conflict management sociodrama deals with the actual conduct of conflict after it has begun and during its course. The fifth kind of reconciliation sociodrama deals with the various concerns that evolve during the termination phase of conflict.

These three phases are parallel to the three parts of Just War Theory, which are usually divided into (a) *jus ad bellum*, which concerns the justice of resorting to war in the first place; (b) *jus in bello*, which concerns the justice of conduct within war after it has begun; and (c) *jus post bellum*, which concerns the justice of peace agreements and the termination phase of war.

4

Crisis sociodrama

"Yitzhak Rabin is dead! He was shot by a fanatic Jew." Looking at one another astonished, we were in shock. We had gathered for a group session in Israel and chosen to focus on the recent assassination of our prime minister just a few days earlier. "What will happen now? What has the world come to? Who was behind it?" We felt insecure and shaken. Someone was chosen to play Rabin and another group member to enact the role of Yigal Amir, the killer. They reenacted the speech, the killing, and some of the afterevents. Then we played a few imaginary scenes with different outcomes. During these enactments, people shared their feelings of loss and bewilderment. Some wanted to talk to the dead prime minister and thank him in person for his efforts to make peace. Others wanted to blame the society for not having prevented it. Then we heard the arguments of the right- and left-wing Israeli politicians who blamed one another for what had happened. At the end of the session, someone said nothing would be the same in Israel anymore after this event. As closure, we sang the song of peace that had been sung just a few moments before the assassination. I think the session helped us all to get some perspective on the sudden tragedy.

The application of crisis sociodrama deals with group responses to catastrophic events of national significance. The word *crisis* means "turning point" and conveys a state in which the whole balance of society is shaken. Classic examples of such significant events that had profound impacts on the citizens of the various countries include the assassinations of President J. F. Kennedy in the United States and Prime Ministers Olof Palme in Sweden, Zoran Djundijic in Serbia, Indira Gandhi in India, Rafik al-Hariri in Lebanon, and Yitzhak Rabin in Israel. Terrorist attacks, earthquakes, riots, and wars are further examples of events that put whole nations into general states of emergency. All of these can be partly or fully explored through crisis sociodrama.

As in crisis intervention, which is used to help a client cope better with a personal tragedy, crisis sociodrama is intended to help the group as a whole cope better with their shared psychological stress. Such common working through of catastrophic events increases the sense of cohesion in a population.

Crisis sociodrama may not be suitable during or immediately after the catastrophic event when people are still overwhelmed by anxiety and the social structure is chaotic. According to Bustos (1990), sociodrama needs a little distance from the real drama, which is so much more encompassing. Within the first days or weeks after the crisis, when there is still smoke from the fire or when the dead are not yet buried, there is little room for such activities. Only at a later stage, when survivors have acknowledged their loss and buried their dead, may sociodrama help them confront and work through their feelings of loss.

Immediately after the event, or within the first three days after the event, it is more helpful to suggest some kind of debriefing activity for the affected population and rescue personnel involved in or exposed to the immediate consequences of the disastrous event. The Critical Incident Stress Debriefing approach (Mitchell 1983) and similar structured strategies are suitable in this early phase to help people reduce their initial distress. Such procedures are not recommended for healing or resolving issues but should be used more as preventive measures to mitigate possible later detrimental traumatic effects on those affected. In most cases, these strategies provide some structure to the initial chaos.

According to Mitchell and Everly (2001), the seven stages of debriefing include (a) engagement, (b) facts, (c) thoughts, (d) feelings and reactions, (e) normalization, (f) education, and (g) disengagement. Debriefing is especially helpful for those immediately affected, allowing them to process the event cognitively and emotionally. At a later stage, people from the periphery of the event may also be invited to share their perceptions and feelings in a more classic crisis sociodrama.

An on-going discussion among trauma experts continues about the extent to which talking about traumatic incidents immediately after the events is at all helpful. Some say that, when survivors recount in detail the terrifying images, these images become even more deeply imprinted in their minds. This in itself might make such images more difficult to erase. Trauma survivors, they say, should instead try to forget as much as they can about the horrible events. Some trauma therapists even go so far as prescribing "forgetting pills" (Propranolol) to dampen the tendency post-traumatic clients have for chilling flashbacks. However, while studies have shown that such a drug reduces PTSD (post-traumatic stress disorder) symptoms, the forgetting pill is criticized on the ground that it medicates away one's consciousness. "It's the morning-after pill for just about anything that produces regret, remorse and pain or gilt," said Leon Kass, chairman of the President's Council on Bioethics.

My experience is that most trauma survivors themselves object to the recommendation that they should intentionally try to "forget all about it." Any such advice is received with skepticism and outright opposition. They respond not only that they are unable to forget about the event but that the "let's get back to normal" attitude (which is so common in society) is equivalent to a slap in the face. In fact, they feel deeply insulted by such a lack of empathy and sympathy, feeling that their experiences are not taken seriously, as if the rest of the world does not believe what they are saying. I have heard from innumerable cases that such a negligent attitude to their trauma has aggravated their sense of being different from others and has contributed to their decision to isolate themselves and not to share their horrible experiences ever with other people. Contrary to the recommendation of forgetting, I feel that, although every trauma survivor has the choice to talk or to be silent, many appreciate being invited to share their experiences. Such an invitation acknowledges that they have been through something terrible and that they have a need to share it with others. As we listen to their stories, we also become affected by their tragic destiny, which in a strange way alleviates their suffering by making the particular events a part of the universal injustices of mankind.

Main stages of crisis sociodrama

The therapeutic aspects of crisis sociodrama are similar to those of psychodrama in general (Kellermann 1992) and to psychodrama with trauma survivors in particular (Kellermann and Hudgins 2000). They follow universal stages of resolution, resembling the process of classical debriefing as described previously with the addition of action techniques and staging.

The process starts with introductory comments by the sociodramatist and a verbal summary of the facts of the event. The event is then recollected and reenacted by the participants, who at the same time are encouraged to talk about their experiences, emphasizing their thoughts, feelings, and physical reactions. At the end of the session, there is a time for sharing in which the sociodramatist sums up what people have said in a simple statement that includes both the vulnerability and the resiliency of the group. The group then ends with suitable closure rituals.

Box 4.1 Main phases of crisis sociodrama

These stages represent the main phases of crisis sociodrama:

1. introduction and warm-up

2. reenactment

3. cognitive reprocessing

4. emotional catharsis

5. sharing and interpersonal support

6. closure and ritual.

These phases also emphasize specific therapeutic aspects during each phase. However, they should be regarded more as an overall guideline than necessary ingredients of a complete resolution process of collective trauma. They rarely occur in the described order, nor are they necessarily activated all together during the same session.

Introduction and warm-up

In the introductory stage of crisis sociodrama, participants are introduced to one another and to the process and purposes of sociodrama. The general boundaries and time limits of the session are clarified, and the sociodramatist gives a short description of the action and role-playing techniques that will be used, if needed. During this initial preparation, there is also a conscious effort to create a secure environment in which participants are free to participate as much or as little as they want.

A suitable warm-up for creating a secure atmosphere is to ask participants to introduce themselves as an imaginary plant. Thus, participants may choose to become a tree, a flower, a bush, a lawn, or anything growing. Reversing roles with the plant puts them in touch with "being" and "becoming" and with the cyclical healing processes of nature. Like everything in nature, people grow and they die; and, like plants, people must be cared for to actualize their potential. Good gardeners know how to care for their plants, to provide them with the optimum environment, with sufficient water and nourishment, and with suitable sun and shade. Having done all that, they rely on the inner growth potential of each plant and hope that it will give flowers in its season. People are similarly in need of such an optimum environment.

However, as the old Chinese Proverb says, "A young branch takes on all the bends that one gives it…" Children are shaped according to the childrearing practices of their caregivers. In addition, any plant will be forever scarred by a sudden calamity, caused either by the cruel forces of nature or by some deliberate or accidental injury. However, as all gardeners know well, many plants have amazing healing potential and tend to recuperate even after severe damage. Similarly, traumatized people find ways to continue their journeys of life after severe psychological traumas.

The purpose of such warm-up activities is not only to give participants a comfortable and safe atmosphere in which to share their collective trauma but also to sensitize the group to the healing forces and seasons of growth in nature and especially to reinforce the power of resiliency in the community. I have found it to be a suitable initial anchor to the resolution of the most frightening traumatic events.

Reenactment

After an initial warm-up exercise or some other less symbolic introduction, the second phase of acknowledgement and reenactment of trauma can begin. During this phase, the traumatic event is recreated within the group and the major facts about the event are shared. Participants are asked to make brief statements about how they were involved in the event or how they heard about it and the various circumstances surrounding the event. For example, if the event deals with a major terrorist attack such as September 11, most participants easily remember where they were when they heard about the event and can share this information with the group. This is the main part of the crisis sociodrama sessions because it includes the actual staging and re-enactment of the traumatic event by the participants who volunteer to play the various roles needed in the drama.

In retrospect, these reenactments with their personal recapitulations often create multifaceted pictures of community coping and reorganization. Such reenactments not only help the group unfold the actual catastrophic event but, more importantly, give opportunities for different group members to show in action what they remember from the event: where they were, how they felt, and how they were able to cope. All this painstaking work will create a new narrative of the event, which has been repeatedly found to be very important as a step in the therapeutic healing process of each and every participant.

If survivors of a trauma cannot by themselves reenact the traumatic event, there can be other, vicarious ways of recapitulation. One very powerful method is the "playback theatre," created by Jonathan Fox (1994). This form of improvisation is devoted to the dramatization of a personal story. Storytellers from the audience come to a special chair just inside the playing area and are interviewed by a conductor. After the story has been told, it is enacted, or "played back," by trained actors who immediately improvise the happenings without any prior rehearsal. Often mime is used, with the addition of musical elements. In the course of such a performance, many people may share their stories and many scenes are enacted, thus revealing the universal collective themes of that particular group. Playback is a remarkably effective method for the collective healing of traumatic community events. Lately, a program has been organized to bring playback theatre to persons affected by Hurricane Katrina in New Orleans and other affected regions.

Repetitive reenactments of traumatic events are both characteristic signs of traumatization and an essential part of most trauma treatment approaches. While habitual repetition compulsion may be understood as the unsuccessful attempt at mastering intolerable stress, the intentional process of remembering, repeating, and working through the trauma provides the platform for most trauma treatment approaches, including sociodrama. Such therapeutic reenactment involves going over the traumatic event again and again to verbalize memories and sensations in every detail and to present in action whatever is impossible to put into words. However, as emphasized by Kellermann (2000), enactment in itself is insufficient to provide any resolution and often needs to be accompanied by other elements, such as cognitive reprocessing of the event.

Cognitive reprocessing

According to Kellermann (2000), most trauma theories view PTSD as a response to the inability of traumatized people to process new information and store it in the memory. The aim of therapy is, therefore, to help them integrate the conflicting information and to construct new meanings of the old and the new (Horowitz 1976; McCann and Pearlman 1990).

The third stage, cognitive reprocessing, provides a new or more thorough understanding of what happened and gives some structure to the chaos that is often the direct result of collective trauma. The goal of this stage is to help participants process their cognitive responses to traumatic loss and their inability to appraise what happened immediately and adequately. When the actual facts are reported in a structured manner within the supportive environment of the group, participants can ask questions about what was done to help and what could have been done differently. Such processes may facilitate not only expressions of grief but also feelings of anger and guilt (Beck 1999). This stage also serves to correct distorted attitudes toward the event, as well as providing a way to explore alternative ways of coping with the loss.

At this stage, people need to face the facts and make sense of what has happened. Because people often play down the importance of these events and deny their significance, this part of the crisis sociodrama forces them to acknowledge what happened. The aim is to assist them in retrospect to say to themselves, "Yes, we lived through it. We suffered. We remember. It happened to others and it also happened to us." Such a gradual increase in self-awareness is often accompanied by emotional catharsis and a powerful discharge of surplus energy.

Emotional catharsis

The fourth stage, emotional catharsis, drains the emotional residue from the trauma. At this stage, survivors should have opportunities to share their feelings in a nonjudgmental, supportive, and understanding manner. Survivors must be permitted to identify their own emotional responses and to relate to the here and now.

During this part of crisis sociodrama, participants separate the past from the present and express their feelings from the event and their current feelings: "How did you feel when that happened?" and "How are you feeling now?" If suitable, some people will acknowledge that "things do get better" with time. However, there is often a variety of other feelings in connection to the event that were not acknowledged earlier but may now be both experienced and expressed. Such feelings may include overwhelming grief, fear, and shame. The sense of humiliation is often a largely neglected sensation (Lindner 2001).

Emotional catharsis is the experience of release that occurs when a long-standing state of inner mobilization finds its outlet in affective expression (Kellermann 1992). For traumatized people with pent-up emotions that have built up like steam in a pressure cooker, such an opportunity to "blow off steam" usually provides some sense of relief. Clearly, survivors of collective trauma need to deal with the event to cope with it. Covering it up and doing something else do not seem to be very helpful in such situations. Brushing feelings under the carpet leaves them lingering like concealed snakes, waiting to bite and poison the person who tried to hide them.

It is wise, however, to be cautious of any unrestrained expression of emotion. Traumatized people are often more fragile and vulnerable than others and have adopted more or less primitive defenses to shield themselves from their overwhelming feelings of pain. The goal is, therefore, to find a suitable combination of detachment and involvement rather than to attain a full-blown and unrestrained catharsis.

Trauma survivors often find it very difficult to share their memories and to talk about what happened to them. When they are able to retell their stories before an attentive audience, they often experience immense relief. Finding a narrative of a difficult life experience is liberating in itself, according to Dori Laub, who gave as an example the testimony of a female Holocaust survivor who seemed to break out of Auschwitz just by talking about her experiences.

Unfortunately, such a sense of release does not always happen as a result of giving testimonies. There are several accounts in the professional literature of Holocaust survivors who kept retelling their stories like a broken record, experiencing no sense of relief from such a repetitive narration. From my experience working with this population, I can confirm this latter skepticism in the automatic cathartic effects of simple narration. While thousands of Holocaust survivors have given videotape testimony for historical purposes, the therapeutic value of such simple recounting of memories is questionable. Apparently, there must be more to the healing of such severely traumatized clients to provide any sustainable change. Today, 60 years after the original Holocaust trauma, we can conclude that such liberation will never occur for many.

What we can do, however, is provide such people with a supportive environment that understands their past and present pain and that is sensitive to their needs. In such an environment, traumatized people are no longer seen as objects being pushed and pulled and shaped by forces outside of themselves. They are rather encouraged to view themselves as active and responsible in constructing their lives and as cotherapists in their very personal journeys of trauma resolution.

As a result, the group leader must choose a suitable balance between support and confrontation that considers the special emotional needs of traumatized people in confronting and avoiding their feelings. Clearly, only when these people have developed sufficient internal control should emotional catharsis be encouraged, and then it should be followed by some kind of communal sharing and interpersonal support.

Sharing and interpersonal support

In the fifth stage, sharing, the focus is on community support to prevent the survivors from isolating themselves or being isolated by the community (Figley 1993). At this stage, the goal is to emphasize universality so that survivors learn that their emotional responses are shared with many others who have experienced similar traumatic events.

It is, therefore, important that every sociodrama session ends with sharing on a deep emotional level by the participants. Such sharing leads to a sense of universality – that we have been through more or less the same ordeal and we have all survived it. It is this feeling of being in the same boat with fellow survivors that helps people cope better with their losses or misfortunes and challenges them to rebuild for the sake of everybody's future.

This stage is also designed to assist survivors in learning new coping skills to deal with their grief. Because various cognitive and emotional stress reactions to the traumatic event have been delayed and are expressed for the first time only at a later stage, it is important that sociodramatists point out that such responses are very common among trauma survivors. In fact, they may point out that typical post-traumatic stress reactions, including nausea, distressing dreams, concentration difficulties, depression, grief, anxiety, and fear of losing control, are normal responses to abnormal events and that such reactions may last from a few days to a few weeks in most people. At the same time, sociodramatists may inform the group of more disturbing responses and make themselves available for individual consultations with participants who have more protracted or severe responses. These participants should also be referred for additional mental health counseling.

Closure and ritual

Closure, the final stage, should include a natural unfolding of events and a smooth termination structure for the group. Suitable closure strategies wrap up loose ends and allow the group to disband with ritual or with tearful farewells.

As described by anthropologists and others (e.g. Johnson *et al.* 1995), rituals contain the basic healing aspects of traditional ceremonies, which have been commonly used since time immemorial by communities around the world to honor their dead and to pray for a better future after having been hit by acts of God. These community ceremonies provide a structured framework for people to make transitions in their lives and adjust to their new circumstances. In the aftermath of traumatic experiences, rituals are also important in providing people with a sense of safety and security and in helping them express their feelings in a symbolic manner.

A powerful structure for such a closure ritual within sociodrama is the ancient Native American ritual, called the "talking stick." An object, originally an oak branch, is passed around the group, designating the holder of the object as the person who has the right to speak. Any object that can be passed around the group may be used. The person who holds the object may say anything to the group. Other group members are quiet when that person is talking, but they may say "Hoh!" if they agree to what has been said. If they strongly agree, they may say "Hoh! Hoh!" However, they may not comment or argue when someone is talking. After the object has been passed around the group once or twice, now warm from being held by so many hands, it may be put in the middle of the room as a tangible symbol and memorial of the group theme.

The talking stick gives each participant the attention of the entire group for a brief moment. As participants speak honestly from their hearts, others listen attentively. The ritual conveys respect for different opinions, permission for free speech, and assurance that speakers have the freedom and power to say what is in their hearts without fear of reprisals or humiliation. The talking stick becomes a "transitional object" that helps the group pass from the action phase to the closure phase. Furthermore, it symbolically objectifies the tragedy, as all persons talk about their own feelings, and thus injects that deleterious content into the tangible object. This sends the indirect message that the issue can be left at some time in the future and that life must go on.

At the very end of the crisis sociodrama, the sociodramatist may conclude the session with some final words. The purpose of such summary statements is to empower survivors and encourage them to move on from being helpless victims to coping survivors. Such transformations may be celebrated in communal forms of therapeutic rituals.

Some survivor groups will need a continuation and a common direction after a sociodrama, and the sociodramatist may suggest suitable shared group activities for the participants after the session. It may be a meaningful commemoration event, such as revisiting the location of the catastrophic event to conduct a farewell ceremony at that location. Family and friends of the missing victims performed such ceremonies at various locations along the empty shores after the terrible tsunami in the Far East.

Other activities may include memorial concerts, booklets, or farewell exhibitions, which bring together those who knew the deceased for a last goodbye. Such activities are frequently conducted in Israel in memory of terrorist victims and have a profound impact on all participants. Especially when the victims are children or youth, such events alleviate some of the grief of the families and close friends and give a meaningful perspective to victims' short lives.

Groups who together have experienced terrorist attacks, been taken hostage, or survived earthquakes, train accidents, sinking ships, fires, and other disasters may profit from such collective acts of mourning and resolution of their common misfortunes (Haney *et al.* 1997).

Example

A recent sociodrama session focused on terrorist attacks around the world. The session was conducted in a large, brightly lit room. Participants usually entered the room in twos, walking quickly to folding chairs placed by the wall and sitting down. There might have been around 60 people in the room. There was laughter and talk and people moved about with purpose. The leader of the group approached some of the new people and introduced herself briefly. After a while, she proceeded to outline the goals of the session and explicitly focused on the emotional consequences of international terrorism.

As the session proceeded, a female survivor of a terrorist bombing recreated the event as she remembered it. She wanted to share with the group how her ordinary journey to work had turned into a nightmare. The entire group was actively involved. A participant volunteered to play the role of the suicide terrorist; others played the roles of victims, survivors, and bystanders.

At the point of the explosion, she described her response as one of shock. The scene contained broken glass and twisted metal. At first, she could not fully comprehend what had happened. The blast was unbearably loud. Her ears went deaf and she was unable to register what happened immediately. Only after a few moments, or hours, did she slowly start to grasp the profound impact of the event; and only then did she start to respond emotionally. Ever since then, she became jumpy when she heard any noise like that. "It's a kind of horror combined with bewilderment," she said.

Immediately after the bombings, she had difficulties falling asleep and kept waking up in the middle of the night. During the day, she felt exhausted. The images of crying and screaming victims haunted her day and night, and her physical pains were a constant reminder of the terrifying incident. She tried to think positive thoughts, such as "I should be lucky to be alive," but was unable to do so.

When she finished her reenactment, there was time for the other participants to tell their stories also. A bystander explained that, immediately after the explosion, there had been first a minute of total silence followed by total panic – screams, sobs, and great confusion. Seven people had died and a hundred injured. Everyone had been terrified when it happened. As they had run to safety, they had seen the many victims and the great destruction.

People on the periphery, not directly hit by the bombings, also shared the effects of the terrorist attack on them. For some of those who had watched it all on TV, these effects were almost inaudible, like background noise, causing fears of new explosions somewhere they might least expect them.

During the replay of the actual terrorist bombing, participants needed to confront the terrorist and ask him why he had done this, what his motives had been. The stand-in terrorist explained where he came from, what his plans had been, and why he wanted to do it: "I want to kill all the Americans, and all the British and all the Zionists…!" he exclaimed. He said that an authoritarian teacher who had blessed him and praised him for his courage had sent him. As a young man who craved status, he explained proudly, he had been chosen from many. He wanted to shape history. Because he did not believe in any real death, there was nothing to be afraid of. Because he believed in an afterlife, which was better than the present life, he had much to win from taking this action.

At the end of the session, the man who played the terrorist was deeply shaken and needed plenty of time for de-roling. Thereafter, the entire group came together in a circle for sharing. This included not only personal feelings but also comments on the political situation and the various global conflicts that seemed to provide a continuous flow of new explosive content.

Retraumatization

The phases of introduction and warm-up, reenactment, cognitive reprocessing, emotional catharsis, sharing and interpersonal support, and closure and ritual constitute a holistic framework for the sociodramatic exploration of collective trauma. When combined with a psychodramatic approach to alleviating the deleterious effects of psychological trauma, as well as with the eclectic utilization of other psychotherapeutic instruments, this becomes a powerful way of helping people cope better with the various catastrophic experiences of life.

This power, however, should be viewed as a two-edged sword, having the abilities both to heal and to harm. Apart from its healing effect, there is always the risk of retraumatization or revictimization in crisis sociodrama.

Possibly, some reenactments of traumatic situations should be avoided altogether if the setting does not give sufficient protection to the participants. I have participated twice in sociodrama sessions that had detrimental impacts on some participants. The first was organized during an open session at a psychodrama congress and the second during a short professional seminar. A very experienced sociodrama director conducted both and the sessions dealt with the theme of the Holocaust. During the sessions, participants were encouraged to reenact brutal scenes from the Holocaust – the terrible selection process at a concentration camp and the release by Allied troops of nearly dead victims at the end of the war. In both sessions, there were participants who were overwhelmed by anxiety, unable at the end of the sessions to recompose themselves and come to terms with their emotional responses. As far as I saw, they were left alone with their distress, without proper closure and reintegration processes.

As I have pointed out before:

> because of their earlier experiences of losing control (over their selves and bodies and environment) and of being manipulated into doing things that they did not want to do, the need of traumatized people for a gentle touch, that recognizes their basic needs of safety, holding and closure, is especially critical. For example, the sociodramatist should make every effort to prepare for the session in terms of explaining what is going to happen at each stage of the process and to get the protagonist's

consent to participate and become involved. Obviously, the golden rule
of client-centered therapy, manifested in the attempt of the
sociodramatist to "follow" the protagonist, rather than to be manipulative and directive, is crucial. (Kellermann 2000, p.35)

Thus it seems that involvement and distance are the two main forces that
evolve around the central axis of balance within each group and each session.
To maintain necessary control, the director should sensitively guide the group
through "tolerable doses of awareness, preventing the extremes of denial on
the one hand and intrusive-repetitiousness on the other" (Scurfield 1985,
p.245).

5

Political sociodrama

When I first began practicing group psychotherapy in a psychiatric ward of a general hospital, I was told there were four subjects that should not be discussed in the group: politics, religion, money, and sex. These subjects would be too difficult for the patients to handle and would only create trouble. It would be much safer, they said, to limit the subjects that were talked about to dreams, relations, memories from childhood, and other such personal issues.

Everything really important and potentially controversial was thus effectively kept out of the group. For example, if one of the group members was an immigrant torture survivor, eagerly awaiting a permanent asylum visa, the group was discouraged from discussing the politics of immigration. If the issue was perpetuated, the client would be advised to discuss this concrete matter with his social worker in another setting. And the man who had lost his job because of some injustice done to him in his workplace should talk to his former employer or to a labor union representative. And the woman who revealed having doubts about the existence of God was referred to her priest to discuss the matter. And if all the psychiatric patients in the group were feeling they were mistreated by society and hospitalized without any real reason, they should bring it up with their families or with the hospital administration, not with the group therapist. In all such cases, the group psychotherapist should tactfully turn the subject matter around and focus on the psychological, and often unconscious, processes within the patients rather than explore what possible outer reasons there might be for their present difficulties.

In contrast, political sociodrama invites participants to explore whatever difficult issues they may have regardless of source. Participants are encouraged to bring up whatever issues are bothering them, including politics, religion, money, and sex, to explore how these issues prevent them from being happy. In fact, political sociodrama encourages participants to explore precisely those social and community issues that they believe restrict their full potential.

Such an approach is based on the assumption that individuals can only be partially responsible for their adjustment to society, which may be too demanding and stressful for many. If this is the case, their various "inadequate responses" may be then interpreted as very normal reactions to abnormal situations. The very purpose of the sociodrama group is then to explore what it is in the *society* that is disturbing and how the community should change to accommodate what people need in better ways. The hope is that when people gather together and feel that they have some power they are more able to make a real difference in their immediate environment. Whatever the results of such explorations are, the very experience of sharing community problems with others makes people more aware of and involved in the social problems of their immediate neighborhoods. Even if not all problems can be immediately resolved, the community support in itself may alleviate some of the corresponding individual problems, sometimes reflected in dreams, parental relations, self-images, and memories from childhood, which then will also find their (almost magical) natural resolution.

Compared with crisis sociodrama, political sociodrama does not respond to sudden and unpredictable global catastrophic events. It is one of many group activities that attempt to resolve long-lasting injustices within a society. As such, the group may deal with social disintegration and inequality as manifestations of social conflicts or injustices as well as the lack of accountability of government institutions. Alternatively, the group may search for ways to improve equal opportunities for everybody. Virtually every significant social debate facing communities nationwide is relevant in such a group.

Political sociodrama may be organized during any public gathering, such as a protest rally or a demonstration. They may be held during an election campaign, at a university campus, in a school, or during any large group meeting in which there is a discussion of public issues. Because sociodrama encourages active verbal and nonverbal participation by all members, it may be more suited for democratic social change and transformation than other traditional methods, such as ordinary public speeches and debates.

Examples of issues that can be explored within political sociodrama include the educational reform movement, the criminal justice system, immigration policies, and antidiscrimination efforts. This approach can also be utilized in urban planning for housing and community development. Inevitably, any such work will give vital inspiration and input to community organizations through interest groups trying to influence decision makers concerning resource allocation and community planning. In many of these issues, sociodrama profitably cooperates closely with advocacy groups, grassroots organizations, legislators, law enforcement, the media, the courts, and other parts of the community that pursue social development.

Such work, however, not only creates a powerful tool for energizing grassroots efforts but also engages various kinds of community leaders and government officials in all its activities, making it more effective and politically significant. A variety of voluntary nonprofit organizations, from religious to secular, may also be invited to contribute their points of view. On college campuses, for example, political activist groups are the natural cooperative partners.

Political sociodrama may also be applied to various socioeconomic issues within trade unions, citizens' rights groups, neighborhood committees, political parties, educational institutions, feminist groups, or other social activist groups. For example, the social class analysis conducted by Monica Westberg and coworkers in Sweden explored the tensions between the working class, the bourgeoisie, and the upper class.

Political sociodrama often has a definite political agenda with a clear ideology and purpose. It is, therefore, natural that most such sessions focus on central political value conflicts, such as the ideals of right and wrong, justice and injustice, fair and foul play, respect and contempt, equality and inequality, altruism and egoism, authoritarianism and democracy, etc. Despite such inherent conflicts, however, it is important that participants strive to meet as equals and give each side an opportunity to present its worldview. In fact, without at least some amount of free speech, as well as basic liberty and equality, political sociodrama is meaningless. This must be a genuine meeting between participants who respect one another and in which they may speak their minds freely without fear of reprisal.

Most political sociodrama in the western world is based on liberal principles and beliefs in democracy and free speech. While it may acknowledge that some social change occurs as a result of conflict, it searches for ways in which social improvement can be reached by peaceful, nonviolent means. In such an atmosphere of gradual social change through dialogue and consensus, it encourages participants to engage in open communication, deliberations, and negotiations rather than in power struggles and violent confrontations. Such sociodrama groups naturally assume goodwill drives people and people can reach consensus with a minimum of friction and coercion. However, other practitioners of political sociodrama may choose to work from a more radical political viewpoint, including Marxist ideology. These radical groups aim for social protest and agitation (Buer 1991; Petzold and Mathias 1982). Sociodramatists identified with this socialist camp usually fight for the working class and minority causes, trying to improve the situation for the weakest and most neglected people in the social hierarchy who are subject to continual injustices and have little or no political power of their own.

The unique quality of political sociodrama is that it draws its theoretical frames of reference from psychopolitics, psychohistory, and political psychology (Kressel 1993). *Psychopolitics* explains politics with psychological theories (e.g. Robins and Post 1997). This field explores both the influence of psychological processes on political behavior and the effects of the political system on the thoughts, feelings, and motives of individuals. Indoctrination, manipulation, and mass communication of a political message are relevant topics for such studies in totalitarian states while characteristic voting behaviors of certain groups of people are relevant fields of study within a democratic system. *Psychohistory*, on the other hand, combines the insights of psychotherapy with the research methodology of the social sciences to understand the emotional origin of the past and present social and political behavior of groups and nations. Its foremost spokesperson is Lloyd deMause from The Institute for Psychohistory, who wrote *The Emotional Life of Nations* (2002).

From a more practical perspective, political sociodrama is closely related to political theatre. It uses a variety of similar approaches, such as image theatre, forum theatre, rainbow of desire, and especially Boal's (1979, 1992) radical theatre of the oppressed (Feldhendler 1992), or Freire's (1999) pedagogy of the oppressed, plus the spontaneous theatre of anarchy (Aguiar 1998). All of these types of theatre attempt to transform the classical elements of traditional theatre in which the audience is passively watching the drama on stage to more active interaction between the stage and the audience to create an ideal form of community dialogue, which is essential for any democracy.

Practice

Political sociodrama follows the same stages as most other action-oriented groups. One obvious difference, however, is that many groups decide their political agenda before the start of the sessions and plan according to these purposes. If, for example, the sociodrama is organized within a school to teach democracy and tolerance, this is clearly announced to the participants prior to the first session. Similarly, if the gathering is a response to a community problem, such as violent riots between various subgroups over perceived injustices, the session is clearly described as a meeting to find a suitable response to this problem.

As a consequence of this clear agenda, the organizers gear their publicity efforts to reach groups believed to have a special interest and benefit in attending. The event is publicized to relevant grassroots organizations and community subgroups, and local politicians may be invited as well. Preliminary meetings with representatives of such groups are very helpful in preventing misunderstandings about the actual intentions of the organizers. Naturally, the political agenda must be shared with all participants prior to the session to ensure no one feels manipulated.

Political sociodrama sessions may last from a few hours to a day or more and generally include any or all of four phases. In the first phase, group members introduce themselves according to the customs of their society. There may then be discussion and clarification of the purpose and general scope of the session. Issues of safety, belonging, and acceptance of subgroups within the large group may also be clarified; and if there are obvious sociopolitical concerns those should be addressed in a straightforward manner in this introductory phase.

Political sociodrama is best managed in a stricter manner than other types of sociodrama. Because of the tension inherent in the various issues raised, the processes that evolve need to be contained so that the group can handle them without too much frustration. Rather than creating a playful atmosphere during the introductory phase, which may be appropriate in other forms of sociodrama, the director should acknowledge the initial difficulties and tensions that often arise when exploring difficult social and political situations and share with the group the need to find a way to work together suitable to all participants. Members of the group may perceive the use of "ice-breakers", and other such strategies that build cohesion within the group and which are often fun and entertaining, as being inappropriate and even manipulative within these serious frameworks. Instead, initial discussions of possible resistance punctuate the seriousness of the issues to be explored and lead to better resolutions at the end of the session when people are faced with the inevitable choice of leaving their destiny to others or taking responsibility for any change they may require from the local or national leadership.

During the second phase, focusing, the sociodramatist may suggest hot political topics from recent newspapers or show a short documentary film on some pressing social issue. Alternatively, if the session is scheduled before or after elections, politicians may give short introductory position speeches to the group. Thereafter, the group may discuss the theme, give some background to the problem, and emphasize the urgency of exploring it at this time. If the group is too large for the active participation of most group members, the leader may divide it into smaller entities to permit more people to express themselves in depth. These smaller groups may then complete specific assignments or discuss problematic situations that are summarized and later brought back to the large group.

In the third phase, enactment, a symbolic situation representing the main theme of the group is staged. This may be a real public event that occurred and that everybody knows about or an improvised presentation of a problematic political situation. The enactment should include the major roles present in the situation and should be played by the actual bearers of these roles (if they are participants in the sociodrama session) who express their own opinions or by other participants who take the roles of the absent important figures.

Participants in each role are initially encouraged to express their points of view, maximizing their ideologies. They are urged to take sides, be opinionated, and express their personal beliefs clearly. Thereafter, they are invited to reverse roles with the other side and repeat the values expressed by the other position. Finally, they are asked to look at the whole situation from outside, as in a mirror. From this more distant perspective, they then express what they see happening and try to find some political solution to the situation. Thus, participants may explore a great variety of positions in a sociopolitical conflict, including tough-minded versus tender-minded viewpoints, conservative versus radical ideas, fascist versus liberal opinions, and fascist versus democratic ideals (Bales 1970; Eysenck 1954), and may be asked to defend their positions.

In sociodrama groups that explore the effects of oppressive regimes and totalitarian political systems, it may be suitable to suggest that group members show this situation in action. Utilizing the psychodramatic technique of "sculpturing," this will concretize the situation and help to focus the session on the various roles involved in the power struggle.

Also in such sessions, group members may be asked to take various central roles in a war scenario, allowing them to face history in the context of facing themselves. In numerous such sessions on the late after-effects of the Nazi regime in Europe during the Second World War, I have found it very constructive to explore in depth the roles of the victim, the collaborator or perpetrator, the rescuer or helper, and the bystander during such times (Kellermann 2004). While these roles are often used to look at certain aspects of the war scenario, none of them are easily delineated and they should not be used in a simplistic fashion. Reality supports the idea that one person may embody more than one role at the same time, especially during the extraordinary chaotic times of war. Thus, there can be a soldier who is both a perpetrator and a victim, as well as being a bystander and possibly a helper, in certain situations. Similarly, a victim can take other roles, depending on the requirements of the situation. We will further discuss the specific roles of the perpetrator (sometimes personified by the "dictator") and of the various victims (or "enemies of the people") in such situations later in this chapter.

After such an enactment, the group needs some kind of closure. The ideals of closure in political sociodrama, however, are not limited to striving for "completion" and "cooling down." As I earlier emphasized,

> I do not think that all sessions must be terminated on an optimistic tone. Some psychodramas that end like fairy tales with the protagonist hero riding off into the sunset after a "perfect victory," giving the illusion of living happily ever after, are deceptive if there has been no significant working through of conflicts. It may be more productive in such cases to introduce a closure scene in which the protagonist recognizes unresolved conflicts, faces difficult situations, or anticipates an uncertain future. Such closure scenes are open-ended, signifying that life itself is open to unforeseen occurrences and that there are no guarantees of future happiness. This thinking assumes that there are no perfect psychodrama sessions, only more or less honest and human ones. (Kellermann 1992, p.157)

Similarly, we may often have the feeling at the end of a political sociodrama that there is much unfinished material that we have not been able to resolve and that we need more time to search for better solutions.

The final phase, sharing, has a special importance in political sociodrama. In this post-activity debriefing stage, participants process what they have learned. However, this is much less personal and emotional than what is common in psychodrama. In fact, according to the alienation principles of Brecht (1963), participants may even be asked to distance themselves emotionally and to think rationally and critically about their experiences.

Brecht's *verfremdungseffect*, translated badly as "alienation effect" or "distancing effect," is introduced in political sociodrama to encourage spectators to respond actively to the theatre production rather than remaining passive spectators. These effects prevent participants from becoming too involved and from identifying too much with their characters. They are instead encouraged to detach themselves from the action and look at what happens from afar, using devices such as mirroring, concretization, and role reversal. This "V-effect" may make things look strange or different and is introduced to open new perspectives and put things in a new light, stimulating people to think for themselves and to pass judgment: "That's not just. This must stop. Let's do something about it!" Thus, spectators who previously felt powerless and alienated become more politically involved in community matters and more motivated to discuss with others what should be done to improve the situation.

During this final phase, as many participants as possible need opportunities to express themselves. They are asked not only to share their thoughts but also to listen attentively to one another, to engage in responsive conversation, and to embark on a creative problem-solving journey that takes into consideration the needs and possibilities of as many parties as possible. The goal, of course, is that this discussion will lead to constructive suggestions for political change that involve social action – whether that action be writing letters to the government, initiating community meetings, or organizing demonstrations – and will inspire people to actual community involvement that goes beyond the scope of this single session.

Example

The play *An Enemy of the People* by Henrik Ibsen (1882) depicts some of the irrational tendencies of the masses and the hypocritical and corrupt nature of the political systems that they support. It also portrays the essence of the terrible communist oppression that existed in many of the former USSR countries not so long ago.

In a political sociodrama session in Bulgaria, one of the participants announced that he had unfinished business with Stalin. Many years earlier, he had intentionally destroyed a statue of Stalin and had therefore been imprisoned for six years. He was now demanding compensation from the present government, but without success.

A member of the group played the role of Stalin, and the man was urged to express his feelings of rage towards the former dictator. After his speech, he again destroyed the statue of Stalin to emphasize his opposition symbolically, and the public gave him a loud ovation. The man clearly needed to get the years of frustration out of his system, and he looked amazingly relieved after saying what was on his mind. That everybody listened to his story and gave him their praise also had a profound impact; it seemed he spoke for everyone when he was finally "standing up to Stalin" without fear. The person playing Stalin said very little and seemed to become a representative for the communist system at large. Although there was no role reversal with the role of the perpetrator, other people shared their life stories, demanding that the figure of Stalin must listen. As the session proceeded and shifted in focus from the man to the population at large, the concept of the "enemy of the people" emerged.

This derogatory term has been a central concept used in Bulgaria and many other communist countries. It refers to political opponents to the governing regime. Such opponents are accused of conspiring against society as a whole. These people become "non-persons," having no human rights of any kind; they are usually imprisoned or driven out of the society and regarded as outcasts. In these countries, there is widespread fear of being designated an "enemy of the people" because such people are marked forever. As in George Orwell's book *1984*, such persons can be sentenced to severe punishments, including death, on the basis of mere suspicion, accused by anyone, even by their own children.

The group was composed not only of actual survivors of torture but also of children of survivors and children of perpetrators, including a man whose father had been in the secret police. As the participants shared these details, it became clear that much of this fear was still present in the large group. While the transition from a totalitarian system to a new democracy had affected the participants profoundly, total freedom of speech was still not something that they could take for granted. At the end of the session, we therefore concluded that the profound wounds inflicted on the population of Bulgaria from these times still needed time to heal. This session, however, had been another step in gaining the courage to speak up and share feelings and thoughts; and, as such, it was a profound manifestation of the right for free speech.

Totalitarian leadership

Any work with people who have been affected detrimentally by an oppressive political system inevitably ends with some general statement of the dangers of totalitarian systems and an effort to understand the enormous power that such systems had and still have over the population at large. Much of this power comes from a thorough understanding of how to control large groups and crowds. If there is anything we have learned from large groups, it is that they may function as a two-edged sword, both for good and for bad.

On the positive side, large groups embody the community spirit of a class, caste, or race of a people. These may be capable of great deeds, such as defending the population from outside threats and taking care of less fortunate members in ways beyond the ability of single persons. Large groups of people form the backbone of society; and, as long as there is government, they have the potential for concentrated benefits and dispersed costs. People, therefore, come together as citizens of a certain country, socialized from childhood to adhere to the agreed-upon rules and regulations of that society.

However, as described first by Mackay (1841) and later by LeBon (1896), people may also go mad in large groups. Crowds of people may become unthinking entities made to commit criminal acts. Self-serving leaders may utilize this human herd for destructive purposes. According to LeBon, the spirit of the masses is controlled with rhetoric about "democracy," "fraternity," and "equality" because crowds tend to think in vivid images illogically connected rather than on the basis of reason. In addition, crowds express exaggerated emotion (of intolerance) and are very quick to take action without coherent thought. An individual who becomes part of a crowd, therefore, tends to lose himself, feeling almost invincible. In our times, Osama bin Laden has employed such principles of mass hysteria with the airplanes and collapsing towers of September 11 to make the masses susceptible to his paranoid messages of hatred and violence.

Such tactics have also been used by unscrupulous political figures throughout history, including Mao Zedong, Joseph Stalin, Adolf Hitler, Benito Mussolini, Marshal Tito, Ceausescu Nicolae, Ion Antonescu, Idi Amin, Ataturk, Francisco Franco, Yakubu Gowon, Radovan Karadzic, Babrac Kemal, Le Duan, Haile Mengistu, Ante Pavelic, Antonio de Salazar, Hadji Suharto, Chiang Kaishek, Pol Pot, Slobodan Milosevic, Marcos Ferdinanc, Batista Juan, Fidel Castro, Augusto Pinochet, Noriega Manuel, Kim Jong II, Muammar Gaddafi, Ayotallah Komeni, the Shah of Iran, and Saddam Hussein. Crowds have been willing to follow them without question and without protest. While not all citizens in these countries view these rulers as murderers and tyrants, many get goose bumps at the mere mention of these names. These rulers have been responsible for numerous unjust, unnecessary, or unnatural deaths, deaths caused by their initiation or intensification of war; by famine, democide (the murder of any person or people by a government), or resettlement; or by the actions of their minions. But while in power these leaders have also been the unifying levers for their groups, defining their collective identity and their common purpose. Any of these figures could be the object of sociodramatic enactment in the countries in which they ruled. Indeed, as a symbolic way of destroying the power of these leaders, the populations of the former USSR and more recently of Iraq destroyed the statues of their rulers in a very sociodramatic manner.

Political sociodrama aims to help people inoculate themselves from being infected by mass psychoses through developing their capacity for critical thought and self-assertion. Such efforts inevitably include understanding and appreciating people's tendencies for dangerous crowd and group behavior. These sociodramas may also include intentional efforts to empower people to stand up for themselves and to give them the courage and the voice to speak up in such situations. Basically, however, all such efforts will inevitably boil down to some kind of political reeducation through the teaching of democracy.

Political reeducation through democracy teaching

Most political sociodrama sessions address alternative political systems than the ones hitherto prevalent within an oppressive country. Within the western world, such alternatives often cover the basics of democracy in one form or another. This is a very natural process because of the increasing global trend towards electoral democracy today, which replaces the earlier communist regimes and other authoritarian systems of government based on dictatorship, dogmatism, and intolerance towards other political parties. As such totalitarian systems are defeated, liberal democracy has become the predominant political system in the western world. For example, the dramatic breakup of the Soviet Union demonstrates an innate and universal yearning for liberty and political freedom in many countries of Eastern Europe. Since then, there has been a global surge of democracy; and for most people of the world today democracy is the prevailing source of political legitimacy.

However, democracy is not something that comes automatically, and education does not apply only to emerging democracies. Education for democracy is just as important in mature democracies, although it is often taken for granted or ignored. Democracy must be regularly taught and refreshed, and political sociodrama may facilitate this teaching and demonstrate the relative worth of democracy in comparison with alternative systems of government. Thus, some sociodrama sessions, especially with youth and young adults, may focus specifically on the ways in which democracy can promote international peace and foster economic growth and prosperity.

Education for democracy is not an easy task; it must be approached in a systematic manner. Making wise electoral choices, understanding and valuing the importance of the rule of law, working cooperatively to improve society, showing tolerance towards political opponents, judging information provided by the media, knowing how to become active participants in social and political life, and a host of other things must be carefully discussed and considered. Some specific forms of political sociodrama may help people master these skills, as well as help them develop the attitudes required of effective democratic citizens.

The particular value of sociodrama in such democracy training is that it seeks to engage people in active, participatory, critical-thinking-based learning, molding citizens most likely to create effectively a better society. Rather than providing a top-down approach with lecturing, sociodrama provides participants with opportunities for cooperation, free speech, role-playing simulations, and other creative methods. When skillfully used, this form of sociodrama may succeed in increasing the development of citizenship skills in the participants and also in increasing their natural commitment to democratic values. In this regard, this method compares favorably to the results of programs relying predominantly on lectures and reading.

However, we must always remember that democracy in itself does not eradicate all inequality in a society; it does not work miracles in terms of social progress. Octavio Paz, the Mexican author and winner of the 1990 Nobel Prize for Literature, said:

> Democracy is no panacea. It is a way of living together, a system to prevent people from killing each other, so that governments can renew themselves peacefully and presidents can enter office by the avenue of the vote. Democracy teaches us how to live together, nothing more. (Speech given at the Nobel Banquet, December 10 1990, quoted in Frangsmy 1991)

Conclusion

The theory and practice of political sociodrama are still in their infancy. To win wider acceptance, political sociodrama needs to be investigated further and integrated into the context of a wider system of community building. It certainly holds special promise within general governmental educational systems, but concrete outcome results from evaluation studies are needed to substantiate the claim that it can make a real difference for its participants.

Until the results of such evaluations are published, a humble goal of political sociodrama may be to begin reversing the political apathy prevalent in many communities. While it may not be automatically obvious that participants in a sociodrama group will become more actively involved in the public and social sphere, we can assume that all sociodrama participation will have some social impact. To say the least, it will certainly increase community involvement and empower its participants to speak up for themselves within a larger context in which they have not previously had the courage to voice their concerns.

6

Diversity sociodrama

In the middle of a group session, an African-American girl put her head on her arm on the table and started to wail, "You don't know what it's like to be black in America!" The group members sat silently, looking at her and at one another with some embarrassment while the girl continued sobbing. When she calmed down a bit, the group leader said:

> No, we do not know what it's like to be black in America. But we know what it's like to be Hispanic, Asian American, and a new immigrant in this country. And we know what it's like to be the only Jew in a group of non-Jews, and we know what it's like to be homosexual in this society, and we know what it's like to have AIDS, and we know what it's like to be a minority that is looked down upon for any reason. We share the pain of all minorities and we realize that we live in a world that is very intolerant towards those who are not like everybody else. Perhaps you would like to share with us a little more about your own situation and thereafter we can all share how it feels to be different in this, or any, society.

This was the beginning of a diversity sociodrama.

Diversity sociodrama deals with how people feel about being exposed to stereotypes, prejudice, racism, xenophobia, intolerance, stigmatization, and negative bias because of their diversity. Common examples involve immigrants, African-Americans, homosexuals, Japanese, Germans, Jews, Arabs, poor, women, elderly, handicapped, unattractive, obese, and many others. As explained in the literature on social diversity, prejudices exist in all heterogeneous populations based on such differences as age, sex, marriage status, wealth, profession, race, nationality, country of origin, socioeconomic status, sexual orientation, culture, religion, political affiliation, and physical attributes such as height, weight, disability, and general outer appearance, as well as many other variables.

Blatner (2006) described a vignette from a sociodrama session that occurred in a graduate-level course on intercultural communication in which students were role playing, using a real-life experience of one of the group members:

> A young man, barely twenty, is sitting in a café talking to a friend. Suddenly, the woman at the table next to him screams, "Faggot! You disgust me!" and throws a gin and tonic on him, drenching his face and shirt. The young man is humiliated, speechless, and looks to the restaurant staff and his shocked friend for support, finding none. The woman, in her 50s, continues raging against gay men. Someone then walks up behind her, touches her shoulder, and says, "I am so angry because I can't find a man of my own." Another person replaces the first one, saying, "I hate myself for sinking so low; I can't stand to see you so happy!" A third student touches the young man and says, as if voicing his inner thoughts, "This is so unfair! You have no fucking right to talk to me like that!" (p.30)

Inviting people to look at diversity (how we are different from one another) is the exact opposite of looking at universality (how we are similar to one another), which is emphasized in psychodramatic sharing. During this end phase of the psychodramatic process, people feel basically similar to one another as human beings, despite all kinds of external differences. Participants of psychodrama are often amazed to learn that they are not the only ones with a certain problem; that they all have had mothers and fathers who were too strict or too lenient; and that they all sometimes feel afraid, sad, proud, or any other ordinary feeling common to all people. In the final analysis, they feel comforted by the realization that, despite all their differences, they are all simply human beings. They even learn they have all felt different from others at one time or another.

In contrast to psychodrama, however, sociodrama focuses specifically on people in general rather than on each person in particular, and diversity becomes the central issue. Throughout the life of the group, the collective is emphasized over the individual and the sense of "we" and "them" is encouraged in favor of "I" and "you." The purpose is to search for answers to the following questions posed by Maslow (1977): "How do we transcend the differences that currently compartmentalize humankind into mutually exclusive, isolated groups who have nothing to do with each other? How do we make contacts across walls separating classes, religions, sexes, races, nationalities, tribes, professional groups, and IQ groups?" (p.15). These profound questions have no easy answers because, as Maslow goes on to say,

> It is difficult for two people to live together, let alone 200 million. Because we are different from each other and have not learned yet to accept these differences, constructing a society in a way to retain our autonomy, free choice, and permission to grow to full humanness will be difficult, and making the best possible compromise under these circumstances will never be a perfectly satisfactory compromise. (1977, p.20)

To bridge such differences, diversity sociodrama recreates and explores universal person perception processes, including stereotypical labeling and trait attribution. Such explorations make clear that we regularly judge others in a highly subjective and often distorted manner. Nisbett and Ross (1980) traced such errors in perception to the cognitive constructs, or schemas, that people employ to make sense of the complex human world around them. However, these constructs are not only based on simple generalizations but also frequently include prejudices and faulty causal attributions of other people's intentions (Heider 1958). Psychoanalysts call some of these faulty perceptions projections, displacements, or transferences of negative internalized representations of figures from the past upon a present person.

As a result of such subjective person perception processes, we often become very judgmental towards others while looking at ourselves as normal. The comedian George Carlin noted that "anybody driving slower than you is an idiot, and anyone going faster than you is a maniac." Rosenberg, in his 2000 book *Nonviolent Communication*, similarly described such tendencies for judgmental evaluations: "If someone pulled out in front of me in traffic, my reaction would be, 'You idiot!' When we speak this language, we think and communicate in terms of what's wrong with others for behaving in certain ways" (p.16). Thus, we can easily see how judgmental thoughts may lead to derogatory evaluation statements, which in turn may give rise to interpersonal conflicts.

Diversity

Diversity sociodrama is based on the simple notion that people are different from one another in many ways, that they like to be with their own kind, and that they find those who are different from themselves difficult to understand.

Nowhere is this more apparent than in gender difference. That men and women are a little different from one another is not something to write home about. That they seem to come from different planets, however, is often overlooked. Gray's (1992) thesis that "men are from Mars and women are from Venus" was therefore a relief for many who had struggled desperately to understand the opposite sex. Similarly, research has found many other reliable differences between various groups of people in terms of how each group thinks, feels, relates, and behaves. Any such diversity naturally creates formidable communication problems. In fact, any variation in culture (language, dress, and traditions), ethnic group (presumed common ancestry), socioeconomic status, opinions, religious beliefs, and many other kinds of differences creates problems in communication. Thus, if members of each group become aware of such basic and inherent differences and learn the language of the other, the understanding between them is greatly facilitated.

This is, of course, easier said than done. In the process of getting "under the skin" of the other person, it is immediately obvious that the attempt to understand that person is more or less based on earlier preconceptions of such a person. One cannot be fully sure that the traits perceived in the other person are based on real traits or on traits one has projected upon that person. Etymologically, the root of the word *prejudice* comes from "pre-judgment" and means that people apply a previously formed judgment to some person without actually knowing that individual. The question then is how can anyone make any impressions of another person without any such previous inferences?

Macrae, Stangor and Hewstone (1996) outlined what is known about stereotyping and tried to answer the following questions: are stereotypes affective or cognitive? Are they in individuals' heads or in the cultural environment? Are they accurate or inaccurate? Do they cause or simply rationalize intergroup discrimination? In each case, research showed that the answer is probably both. While they concluded that multilevel integrative theoretical approaches that can accommodate the interactivity and complexity of stereotypes are not yet fully developed, they provide clear statements of these major unresolved issues.

Because any person perception is based on some form of generalization, people need to be aware that they may be basing their appraisals on faulty assumptions and stereotypical labeling rather than on real and authentic views of the other people. For example, when a man tries to understand a woman, there is always a certain amount of ambiguity as to his ability to understand someone so different from him. To understand what a woman really thinks and feels, he has to reverse roles with the woman for an extended period of time and fully "become" a woman in all aspects of life, like the male actor who takes a female role. However, while this makes it easier to look at the world from the perspective of women, there is still much that remains beyond reach; and it is still impossible to generalize such an understanding to most other women. This leaves us with the distinct feeling that, because it is so difficult really to understand another person or another group of persons, it may be better to take a very humble position regarding person perception. Perhaps it is necessary to appreciate that there are basic differences that will never be bridged and that we may have to live with our biases.

The following is an exercise that explores this person perception process in action, looking also at how we judge others and make sociometric preferences from these judgments. Participants stand opposite one another in pairs. They keep quiet during the entire exercise and share with one another or the group only at the end of the whole process. They may then choose another partner and go through the same process again. The leader gives the following instructions slowly, letting each person contemplate for a few moments between each direction.

1. Look at the other person.

2. Try to find out who the other person is.

3. Look only at objective and descriptive things.

4. Try to make a judgment and infer from these cues about the personality of the other; e.g. if the other person wears glasses, does it mean that he/she is intelligent?

5. Try to empathize with him or her. What does he or she feel and think?

6. How do you feel when you take the role of the other?

7. Is he/she similar or different to you in this respect?

8. Do you get a positive or a negative attitude to the person now?

9. Do you want to get closer or more distant?

10. Please show this in action.

There are many similar exercises that may be used in groups to explore cultural and religious diversity. For example, the Irish Network for Nonviolent Action Training and Education has devised some active and experiential warm-ups, including simple role-playing exercises that illustrate the diversity conflict in Northern Ireland to people who are not familiar with this conflict. In one such role-play, one person takes the role of a Protestant and the other the role of a Catholic. The pair engage verbally with each other on the issues important to each one in those roles; they try to express how they feel, why they are dissatisfied with the other party, what their dream is for the future, and so on. When they are finished, they share their experience and discuss the underlying reason for why people who are different have so many difficulties getting along with one another. They usually find that much of the problem stems from the ethnocentric tendencies of people.

Ethnocentrism

When individuals look at the world from their own individual perspectives, as if they are each the center of the world, we describe them as "egocentric." Similarly, when several people look at the world from their own cultural perspectives, as if they were the center of the world, we call them "ethnocentric." The various expressions of such group narcissism are the subject of all diversity sociodrama.

Ethnocentrism seems to be a universal trait of most societies. According to Festinger's (1954) social comparison process, people tend to move into groups of similar opinions and abilities and move out of groups that fail to satisfy this need for self-affirmation. In general, people feel that their own country, their own religion, and their own cultural heritage are the superior ones. When people from different countries meet, they each usually boast of their country's achievements as an expression of national pride. Croatians boast about their achievements since the war, Koreans about their new cars, and Italians about their food. For each of them, these achievements are not only admirable and special but the "best in the world." As a result, they prefer their own folk music, their own food, and their own customs and traditions. At international congresses, they stand up enthusiastically to represent their own countries, and at the Olympics they cheer for their own athletes. When one of their own scientists gets a Nobel Prize, they feel proud, as if some of the glory rubs off on them. Most importantly, however, each group feels a deep sense of loyalty towards their own ethnic group and pledges allegiance to their own country. Such belonging defines the very essence of who they are. With the exception of some countries, such as Germany after the Second World War, citizens everywhere have such deep nationalist and ethnocentric feelings.

The funny thing, however, is that when we inquire a little more about any such loyalty, pride, and belonging we always find that they can be further differentiated into smaller units. For example, I met an Italian man who presented himself as being European but who still felt prouder of being "a real Italian." After some time, however, he admitted he was really more of a Corsican than an Italian and that he did not have much in common with those from other provinces. Then it became apparent that in Corsica there were further differences between those who live in the north and the south and between those who live in the city and in the countryside. Because he lived in Bastia, he felt very different from the farmers in Bonifacio. Then he admitted there were major differences between those who were rich and poor and those who were members of one family as opposed to those who were members of another family. "Since centuries," he explained, "these different families never got along with one another." Then he continued to elaborate that the other family would cook a strange kind of pasta, while his family would eat *cannelloni a brocciu*, which was "the best pasta in the world." I felt as if I were listening to the preludes of *Romeo and Juliet*.

As a result of such local patriotism, the original feeling of national ethnocentrism lessens as we descend through the hierarchy of subgroups in the society. Solidarity and understanding seem to be a matter of gradient: Italians will certainly have a deep understanding of one another, but Corsicans have an even deeper understanding, and so on. That is probably why the first question we ask one another when we meet for the first time is "Where are you from?" It helps us to categorize the others quickly in a certain geographic location, to make a swift overall judgment, and then to determine immediately their distance to ourselves.

Ethnocentrism, however, not only influences our passive positioning vis-à-vis others but also has serious consequences for our active involvement in violent conflicts, as illustrated by the following example. Hearing about two men fighting down the street is meaningless to us. We do not know who they are, nor do we know what they are fighting about. But if we learn that one of the combatants is someone we know and he is fighting someone we do not like we suddenly get excited and emotionally involved. In some cases, we even consider taking part in the fight ourselves out of loyalty and identification with the one fighting on "our side." If we do so and are then asked why we interfered, we say, "He would have done the same for me."

Because people judge others from their own perspectives and are attracted by similarities rather than differences, they inevitably look at everybody else as strangers. At best, these strangers are difficult to understand. At worst, they are threats to the unity of the tribe and become our enemies.

When different cultural groups meet, the early fascination usually wears off quickly, and people from the other group become increasingly frustrating. Tensions slowly arise, and there will be some friction concerning norms and regulations. This usually results in the *majority* trying to enforce its own customs and traditional norms upon the minority. Such norms include dominant values about how people should behave to "fit in" and be accepted in the group. This socialization process works on all levels, helping people identify with the larger community and become accepted as full members in that society. While this creates a good feeling of commonality and together-ness for those who conform, those who do not or who are a minority, having other values and norms, are silently ousted. Sooner or later, individuals in such minority groups become "one of them."

Ethnocentrism is self-perpetuating. In a process described as group polar-ization (Sunstein 1999), the more that separate groups indulge in themselves, the more they feel different from others, and the more they take more radical and extreme positions than before. Because people tend to be more confident and more extreme in their opinions after having expressed their views to their own people, we can observe how racist groups become more extreme as a result of their intragroup mutual reinforcements. We may, therefore, assume that different ethnic groups, which live in proximity to one another, will clash sooner or later.

Multicultural societies emphasize the need to find a suitable balance between assimilation (unity) and pluralism (diversity). Assimilation means that there needs to be a common ground (such as one language) among all the diverse people who live in one place. Pluralism, on the other hand, means that there should also be ample room for individuality (such as the freedom to practice one's own religion) within such a "fruit salad" model of coexistence. Sometimes, these two models are difficult to combine, and the people and the governments always choose to emphasize either one or the other. Naturally, because there is a price to pay in both forms of solutions, neither way is perfect.

Let us take America as an example. While there is generally a generous attitude toward immigrants, there are implicit and explicit expectations for everyone who comes to become "American." This means that they must participate in American life: learn America's language, history, and customs; absorb America's Anglo-Protestant culture; and identify primarily with America rather than with their countries of birth.

> We must work to see that our diversity always be a New World symphony, not an Old World cacophony. Our melting pot must create the richest and most varied republic the world has ever seen and never turn into a toppling tower of Babel. (Simon 2005)

Other countries, such as Canada, allow for more pluralism and encourage their citizens to retain their cultural heritage while also being (or becoming) citizens of those countries (e.g. Canadians).

How to manage diversity

At worst, diversity conflict may cause open clashes, war, and even ethnic cleansing. Diversity in itself, however, does not automatically lead to violence. In an extensive study of the effect of social pluralism (ethnic, religious, and racial differences) on violence, Rummel (1997) concluded that:

> where political power is centralized around a trans-plural group, such as a military junta or monarch, or trans-plural ideology, such as communism or fascism, then violence is highly likely, regardless of what plural units may or may not exist. And where power is centralized, non-democratic, and highly dependent upon one's social group membership, such as ethnicity or religion, then collective violence is also highly likely. (p.173)

Even if all diversity conflicts do not always result in violence, they invariably lead to intergroup tensions; and because these in themselves are so destructive for any society there is always a question of how to manage them in an effective manner.

The professional literature on how to manage diversity is rich and instructive (Baytos 1995; Gardenswartz and Rowe 1998; Hayles and Mendez-Russel 1997). O'Byrne (2005) presented an extensive recent overview of the current state of cross-cultural training in the mental health domains. There are also grassroots, advocacy, and political groups promoting cultural or diversity issues; and organizational development institutes and theatre companies offering diversity training seminars to the public. Many of these programs use sociodramatic methods, various role-playing elements, and other action methods originally created for psychodrama. However, as a result of increased specialization, such institutes today apply their skills to specific populations or focus their work on specific diversity problems, such as those that explore the problems of gender, sexual orientation, harassment, race, disability, or culture. For instance, organizational consultants may teach members of an organization to utilize its diversity better, to manage diversity crises, or to prevent open conflict between its various cultural subgroups within the workplace. They have found that managing an increasingly diverse and multicultural workforce is connected to employee satisfaction. Diversity awareness and training have, therefore, become more common in today's ever-evolving marketplace. Within such a workplace setting, the goal is to build an atmosphere in which differences are not only acknowledged but also appreciated and where all employees and all customers are treated with equality and respect.

To maximize the benefits of diversity management, many of these programs emphasize one or the other of the following recommendations:

1. The contacts between the diverse populations should be as rewarding as possible.

2. There should be some basic regulations and social norms (e.g. of equality) established.

3. There should be extra sensitivity to the hurt self-image of minority populations.

4. The learning experience should be based on cooperation and interdependency rather than on conflict and competition.

Diversity sociodrama tries to implement these recommendations within its own strategies and methods.

In all this work, diversity sociodrama tests the personal position of the sociodramatist like no other form of sociodrama, psychodrama, or group work. Any of the various diversity themes are relevant for the sociodramatist, who is immediately identified as a subjective partner in the explorations. The sociodramatist's own preferences, prejudices, and opinions are invariably expressed either directly or indirectly in this work. Therefore, group leaders of diversity sociodrama must adopt a very special cultural identity balance. They must be firmly based in their own cultural identity on the one hand, and on the other hand they must have a deep knowledge of the other cultures present in the group. Most importantly, however, they must take the position of cultural relativism, which means that any individual human's beliefs make sense only in terms of that person's own culture.

Participants who have grown up with more than one cultural identity have a special auxiliary function in diversity sociodrama. These people may have been born in one country and immigrated to another country or may have parents from two different cultural backgrounds or religion (e.g. a Serbian father and a Croatian mother, an Arabic mother and a Jewish father, etc.), as is described in *Mohammed Cohen* (Kayat 1981). As a result, they speak more than one language and are familiar with both cultures "from within," making them invaluable "bridge builders," facilitating communication between members of both cultures. Often, they are the only individuals who can genuinely look at both cultures without bias. In addition, they often have personal interests in bringing both cultures together and invest considerable energy into such efforts. Because some of these multicultural individuals have experienced these double identities as being complex and frustrating, the sociodrama groups reframe this situation as a valid asset to the group. These individuals provide the group with not only two separate and different per-spectives but also a conviction that a combination between them is really possible. An extreme example of this multicultural heritage was manifested in a woman who had a German Nazi father and Jewish Holocaust survivor mother. She had suffered tremendously in bringing these two opposing iden-tities together; yet, in a mixed second-generation group, she was the only person who could genuinely understand both sides of the spectrum and struggled to make the other participants understand one another.

The process of diversity sociodrama

While it is applied differently within various settings, diversity sociodrama typically progresses through seven phases:

1. warm-up

2. group demography

3. focusing

4. enactment

5. resolution

6.   closing ritual

7.   sharing and processing.

Warm-up

In the warm-up phase, the primary task of the sociodramatist is to build an atmosphere of both group cohesion and group conflict through the playful development of intergroup tension. This may be done by using some of the following simple ice-breaking exercises that may help the group gradually to focus on diversity as a source of intergroup conflicts.

Participants may walk around the room slowly and then quickly, trying not to bump into each other. After a while, they are instructed to bump into one another deliberately with their shoulders. Among other things, this warms the group up to the issue of "clashing" and to physical encounters. It may also break some barriers to physical contact. Thereafter, the entire group may stand in a large circle and then each person in turn may say "Hello," introducing themselves with their names and an accompanying movement. The group responds by imitating or mirroring each person's introduction, giving all participants the chance to be seen by the entire group and to see how the group views them. After the last introduction and while still standing, all participants join shoulders, pressing hard inwards without breaking the circle. Each inward push may be accompanied by hard breathing, grunting, or other such sounds indicating the energy and concerted effort each individual is expending in this team effort. Such instant cohesion-builders emphasize the inherent structure and power of the group as a whole.

Group demography

When the group has been prepared and has warmed up to one another, it is time to look at the composition of the group. This includes an extensive demographic investigation of the group done according to specific criteria. By using spectograms, the sociodramatist can collect a mass of descriptive information quickly. Spectograms work by having participants place themselves on an imaginary continuum according to their answers to questions the dramatist asks. For example, participants may rapidly group themselves according to differences in sex, age, height, place of birth, religion, marital status, ethnicity, or any other variable that may be relevant, including some which focus on opinions. Such repeated group divisions help loosen rigid perceptive patterns and create a kind of chaos of nondescription and non-categorization, which stimulates partial regression to nonverbal modes of person perception and intra-group variability.

Similar to any study of individual differences, group demographic spectograms may be based on nominal (yes/no, either/or) measurements of mutually exclusive categories (e.g. male or female), on ordinal (more or less) measurements (e.g. liking), or on interval measurements (e.g. age). They may focus also on interests, abilities, motivations, personality, education, skills, or hobbies or on traits, such as emotionally expressive–reserved, emotionally stable–neurotic, dominant–submissive, cheerful–depressed, outgoing–shy, dependent–independent, trustful–suspicious, conventional–unconventional, or any similar continuum of personality traits.

To emphasize the positive element of being different, the group may focus on ways in which each person is "special." Participants may be asked to mention something about themselves they believe is very different from everybody else in the group. For example, one person may be the only one who has only four fingers on one hand, someone else is the only one who has more than ten brothers and sisters, and a third person is the only one who speaks Swahili fluently. The group leader may reinforce the positive element in being different by asking the group to respond to each special thing with a vocal expression of praise or with applause, creating a sense of appreciation of differences, at least on a superficial level.

Various sociometric exercises may also be used, either in action or on paper, to explore the interpersonal distance, closeness, and neutrality between people. One such exercise involves people imagining they are swimming in a magnetic pool, being drawn towards those who are similar and being repelled by those who are different. Then they reverse the process to see what happens.

Focusing

To focus on a specific theme, the group leader may suggest participants choose someone in the group whom they feel is most similar to themselves and someone they feel is most different. While this exercise is not a sociometric identification of stars, isolates, and possible minority subgroups, it may extrapolate the group norm from the various criteria used and lead the group towards looking at divergence as deviance and uniformity as normality. A discussion of what it means to be "normal" and "deviant" in this specific group may then follow and, using a spectrogram of "normality," may further concretize this point.

These exercises usually stimulate sufficient material to focus on specific diversity issues. The group will profit from verbalizations of the phenomena revealed to the director. These observations may be formulated in terms of the shared central issue or concern of the group or in terms of more hidden inter-group conflicts. Regardless of the terminology used, group members should feel the central issue of divergence deeply and acknowledge the urgent need to explore it further.

As a result of these focusing exercises, the group may need to explore what one subgroup thinks about another group. The "behind-the-back" technique, originally created to provide individual feedback, may be used here for group generalizations. A specific subgroup, such as all men, sits with their backs to the other subgroup, all women. The women are asked to talk openly about the men, as if the men cannot hear what they say. The women are encouraged to say whatever they like, including what they would not normally reveal when the men are listening. When the women have finished talking, the men turn around and respond to what they have heard. Then, the reverse is done. The more difficult the diversity issues and the smaller the size of the minority group, the more explosive the results of all such focusing exercises will be. Therefore, the sociodramatist must ensure that sufficient trust has been estab-lished in the group and that appropriate follow-up is completed to contain the evolving emotional responses to any such explorations.

Enactment

In the central phase of enactment, the major roles, positions, and interrelation-ships of the chosen issue and the conflict are identified. Thereafter, a charac-teristic diversity scene with conflict is enacted in which a deviant actor fails to meet the shared expectations of the group. People may present situations in which they were exposed to prejudice or racism because of their diversity. The African-American woman mentioned at the beginning of this chapter enacted a job interview in which she was refused employment because of the color of her skin. Another participant showed how people responded to him as a homosexual, another as a Muslim. Various participants took roles in the sociodrama and were asked to verbalize what was going on inside them, between them, and outside both groups. This phase of sociodrama is largely based on psychodramatic role-playing principles and techniques and will not be further described here.

In a diversity sociodrama in Vukovar, Croatia, the following situation was recently enacted. A child walked with his mother and grandmother to register in kindergarten. As they walked through the entrance gate, the grandmother, who was Croatian, stated firmly that the child naturally had to register in the Croatian school and not in the Serbian one located just opposite this school. The mother, however, who was more liberal and wanted Croat and Serb children to play together to defuse some of the tensions from the war, accepted the advice of the grandmother hesitantly. She said, "Yes, but how will Croats and Serbs learn to live together, if we already at this age separate them?" The five main roles with their various expectations were then put in character: the Croat, the Serb, the child, the grandmother, and the society, each asserting its main messages. Trying out the possible solutions, the group suggested that it would be nice to have a mixed kindergarten with all children playing together; but everybody realized this would be impossible in this time and age. During the sharing, we discussed the prevalence of mixed marriages in this society. However, most of the participants felt that such marriages would be rejected by both societies because the time was not ripe for a pluralistic society.

Working through and resolution

After the enactment, the group does an experimental search for alternative solutions, which may be found in a promotion of pluralism and the possible coexistence of opposites. Following their own convictions, sociodramatists may focus on either one or all of the following four strategies of conflict management: emotional, intrapsychic, interpersonal, and group-as-a-whole strategies, which will be fully described in chapter 7. Here, each will only be briefly exemplified with an action-oriented exercise.

EMOTIONAL

In this first level, and to intensify further and maximize the confrontation, one group is instructed to say "Yes!" while the other group is instructed to say "No!" Participants use the strength of their group to win over the other group; the dramatist urges them to shout, use physical power, and let out all their pent-up hostilities towards the other group. The rationale behind this exercise is that, when both groups have exhausted their energies and "fought their fight," they will be more open to intrapsychic group work.

INTRAPSYCHIC

During the intrapsychic (perceptual) level, each group stands opposite the other and first verbalizes and vents their stereotypical views about the other group. For example, if the central issue deals with male–female prejudice, women standing together may say, "All men are chauvinist pigs!" The men may respond saying, "All women are hysterical." Being permitted and encouraged to "talk for the group" and to maximize generalizations of their attitudes helps to diminish personal responsibility and allows prejudice to be more easily expressed. To look at the issue from the other point of view, both groups may later be encouraged to reverse roles and express some of the views held by the other position. The main objective of such a role reversal is to explore perceptual distortions and stereotypical attribution of traits from the position of the other. It is sometimes easier to see oneself from a new perspective, which may modify whatever erroneous conceptions one may have had earlier. As a result, there is ideally a shift in perception, which includes this new perspective.

INTERPERSONAL

A symbolic wall is built between both groups to concretize the intergroup conflict and to facilitate active and experiential exploration of the interpersonal field between both groups. The wall functions both as a sign of territorial privacy and as a protection of personal integrity, like a fence between good neighbors. However, it is also "common property," a potential source of disagreement and a concretization of the difficulties between them. As such, it becomes an obstacle for spontaneous interaction and direct communication. To explore the areas of coexistence and to facilitate nonviolent communication between the parties over the imaginary fence, the sociodramatist may choose to use mediation skills to help the participants work out a suitable agreement. The group is finally urged to decide what they want to do with the wall – build it higher, leave it as it is, or tear it down – symbolizing the various solutions to conflict.

GROUP-AS-A-WHOLE

Both groups are instructed to enter into a competitive game; the winning group is the one that has more chairs on its side of the room at the end of the game. Participants are thus confronted with their individual responses to a contest situation as well as with their identification with their group and utilization of the group as a whole for cooperation. Thereafter, and as a contrast to such competitive games, the group is encouraged to play a non-competitive game based on cooperation, such as one of the new games that do not end in victory or defeat (Orlick 1982; Sobel 1983).

Closing ritual

Towards the end of the sociodrama, when conflicts are well clarified and the possible solutions exhausted, the actual relationship may be confirmed through a closure ritual, such as a live sculpture, a song, or a moment of silence. If the groups have reached a satisfactory agreement, they may close the encounter by shaking hands, smoking a peace pipe, or signing a peace treaty. Such ceremonies help the group to announce their agreement openly, to leave the conflict behind, and to move on to future cooperation.

Sharing and processing

Each sociodrama calls for plenty of time for sharing and processing at the end of the session. Because of the painful personal material that has been expressed in the earlier phases, the group now needs to process the session cognitively in a more distant manner. It is preferable during this phase to ask group members to sit in a circle. Because the circle underscores the equal status of each participant and facilitates communication between everybody, it provides a suitable framework for the discussion of diversity issues and puts the earlier diversity criteria into a new perspective.

This may also be the right time for the group leader or one of the participants to connect the focus of the session to actual diversity issues presently being discussed in society, such as the public policy on immigration. This may lead some members to become more actively involved in such issues within their own community.

Conclusion

As the world becomes smaller, the opportunities and challenges for intercultural exchange have increased, leading to either collisions or mutual exchanges and enrichment. Diversity sociodrama may provide new ways to explore such challenges and be an alternative to the wide variety of diversity training methods available.

We have hitherto talked about diversity mainly as a problem. However, according to Volkan (2002), most people can enjoy human diversity when they are not preoccupied with the anxieties associated with the preservation and maintenance of their own large-group (or ethnic) identity. Diversity sociodrama may create opportunities for warm, spontaneous, passionate encounters between people from totally different backgrounds who would never meet under other circumstances. Having people from different backgrounds together within one group may become an enormous stimulus to growth, interpersonal learning, and network building. Through the unique cultural background of each person, participants have a chance to get to know something different that may be truly enriching. At the very least, diversity in itself makes the group experience more exciting and interesting, providing the impetus for the growth of something that is beyond our own imaginations.

Diversity sociodrama may also give people a unique opportunity to share their own ethnocentrism without encountering prejudice and open hostility. At such moments, diversity sociodrama may lead to the conclusion that generalizations have little or no basis in external reality, thus facilitating personal changes of attitudes. If, however, diversities are real, participants in sociodrama may become more tolerant of those differences (Amir 1976). Such tolerance comes from the realization that not everyone who looks, sounds, and thinks differently from us is bad or dangerous; that other people have their own rights and needs; and that we need to learn to respect people as they are.

In addition to these goals, diversity sociodrama tries to go beyond external cultural and religious diversities to find a common ground around the fight against prejudice itself. The former president of the United States, William J. Clinton, expressed this vision very succinctly:

> The real differences around the world today are not between Jews and Arabs; Protestants and Catholics; Muslims, Croats, and Serbs. The real differences are between those who embrace peace and those who would destroy it; between those who look to the future and those who cling to the past; between those who open their arms and those who are determined to clench their fists. (Speech delivered on December 22, 1997 to the people of Sarajevo at the National Theatre Sarajevo, Bosnia-Herzegovina, Public Papers 1997, p.1814.)

Most of us would probably agree with these words.

Clearly, however, sociodramatists cannot make any serious claims of being able to make people more tolerant towards one other; it is impossible simply to ask people not to be ethnocentric. What sociodrama can achieve is the exploration of our biased perceptions within a supportive environment and encouragement to participants to share the pain involved in being the target of stereotypic labeling. When this happens in public, there will be more awareness and, I hope, more sensitivity for such issues in the future. In addition, participants will become more aware of their tendency toward ethnocentrism and their stereotypical labeling of strangers. This may make them more humble when encountering others and make intercultural encounters less frustrating. Finally, as this process develops, participants may find a suitable balance between seeing the riches in adding other perspectives while still being proud of who they are and appreciating their own unique assets and originality.

Still, if none of this works, and because racism is still an urgent problem in many countries, diversity sociodrama will underscore the importance of creating public policy regarding the open expression of prejudice and racism. Such public policy should ensure that extremists cannot abuse the right to free speech to stir up racial tensions and that laws of incitement against any minority should be strictly enforced.

Postscript: the wall of separation

The Berlin Wall has been torn down; the racial segregation system of apartheid in South Africa has been dissolved. Yet, in other parts of the world, new walls are being built to separate people from one another because they cannot live together in peace. The recent security wall in Israel is such an example. It has indeed provided a sense of security for the Israeli population, but it has created frustration for the Palestinian people. However, the wall may be the first step towards a solution to the Middle East conflict because more and more people, including myself, believe in the solution of the "two states for two peoples" formula. While it may not be the ultimate solution, it seems to be the only one with a chance of succeeding right now.

This solution is built on Moreno's sociometric concept of the "saturation point," which explains one of the causes of intergroup conflicts (1953, p.560). Based on the assumption that when two different cultural groups coexist in physical proximity and when their members are in a continuous process of interaction they will invariably clash, the saturation point is the size of the minority group that the majority group can absorb without producing social tension and wars between the two (Moreno 1943/1972). In simple terms, too much diversity makes for social tension. Thus, the solution is to have more or less segregated societies. In opposite terms, there must be sufficient commonality and homogeneity in a group for it to develop cohesion, which of course is the basic prerequisite for any working group.

This is common sense, you might say; but it has profound consequences for the world we live in and the groups we attend. We seem to tolerate only a certain amount of divergence in the groups we choose to join. When the saturation point is exceeded, usually some kind of implosion or explosion occurs, causing the groups to fall apart and new groups with greater cohesion to form.

A political solution to the problem of how to live together with as little friction as possible despite considerable diversity may be found in the Swiss canton system, which promotes both separation and decentralization of power. Although Switzerland is made up of several different ethnic groups – Germans, French, Italians, and Rhaeto-Romanic – they have lived in prosperity and peace for many centuries. Whenever conflicts have arisen between these language groups and between Catholics and Protestants, the Swiss have resolved the conflict by allowing each of the warring groups to govern itself. Thus, single cantons have been divided into half cantons, new cantons have been formed, and border communes have opted to leave one canton to join another. In this way, the Swiss have developed a system that permits people of different languages, cultures, religions, and traditions to live together in peace and harmony, making the Swiss system particularly well suited to ethnically divided countries. This system may hold some fundamental truth for all of us.

7

Conflict transformation in sociodrama

In earlier chapters, we discussed the theory and practice of sociodrama as it is applied in situations of crisis, political upheaval, and diversity. All of these applications may be seen as preliminary phases of escalating tensions, which instigate some kind of interpersonal conflict if they are not resolved. Man-made trauma provokes frustration and sometimes a wish for revenge, inequality leads to power struggles, and diversity creates intergroup tensions. In the present chapter, we will therefore develop an integrative approach to conflict transformation, which is relevant to the practice of sociodrama.

A sociodramatic conflict transformation strategy differs significantly from classical psychodrama. In psychodrama, antagonists are usually absent from the session and stand-in group members take their roles. In sociodrama for conflict transformation, the real antagonists are invited to the action space. In fact, many protagonists from one group and antagonists from the other group usually present their problems within the same session. The main difficulty is that protagonists and antagonists do not get along very well. At best, they have a minor dispute. At worst, they are at war with one another.

It's a familiar situation. Because, motivated either by national aspirations or by personal drives, people throughout history regularly and repeatedly light the torches of war as a collective consequence of their disputes. Entire societies create and recreate tragic scenarios of hatred and revenge. Intergroup discrimination, riots, terrorism, and violent hostilities form a constant mix of the daily international news reports. What is the function of sociodrama in such situations?

Sociodramatic conflict transformation may be a powerful auxiliary method for conflict resolution and negotiation strategies used all over the world. Because it is based on playful interaction, role-playing, and simulation of conflict situations, it allows the participants to search for solutions in a nonthreatening and experimental environment. In such a protected setting, this kind of sociodrama can provide creative solutions to conflicts that have hitherto been difficult to resolve. At the very least, it will open up an alternative platform of interchange to violent warfare, which is badly needed in many countries of the world. As opposed to some systematic and hard-line negotiation or mediation strategies, sociodramatic conflict transformation proposes a softer approach to handling, encapsulating, transforming, managing, and digesting conflicts. Because no single approach can provide the best (re)solution to a conflict and some stubborn conflicts will remain unresolved, we sometimes have to learn to live with a conflict and be satisfied that it has become a little less malignant and violent than before.

Conflict and hostility

"Hostile attitudes between groups, sometimes leading to aggression, are one of the world's most serious problems. Psychological research so far has succeeded in explaining it, but not in curing it" (Argyle 1991, p.23). Although some people feel that group psychotherapists should not meddle in global sociopolitical matters, others say it is impossible to conduct any therapy without taking universal intergroup conflicts into consideration. From my experience in Israel, I agree with the latter view. When daily preoccupation centers on the stress of physical survival, other concerns lose much of their urgency. In places where people are faced with violent intergroup clashes on a daily basis and where there is increased polarization between various subgroups of society, conflict transformation becomes a task as urgent and important as helping survivors cope with their traumatic experiences.

Moreover, conflicts are brought into every group situation at some point when participants reveal their social identities and start to mirror others and be mirrored by them. As interpersonal relations develop, people are naturally prone to reenact some of the cultural stereotypes and hostilities of the society in which they live, giving rise to scapegoating, fight–flight, or any of the other familiar manifestations of group conflict that reflect the society at large. As Powell (1989) pointed out, "The small group carries in its foundation matrix the destiny of all mankind, with polar opposites of love and hate, integration and destruction and life and death" (p.278). If we as sociodramatists can help to prevent, or to manage, some of the underlying conflicts causing tension, there may be less traumatization and less need for crisis intervention.

Though Moreno (1953) suggested some possible preconditions for a more peaceful coexistence, his theories cannot be regarded as a sufficient basis for sociodrama; they neither explain the development of social conflict in a consistent manner nor formulate clear principles to guide practitioners in their efforts to resolve conflicts. The literature on intergroup conflict in sociology, social psychology, and anthropology, however, is sufficiently rich to provide a strong theoretical foundation for conflict transformation in sociodrama. Conflict is a key explanatory variable utilized by such classical social thinkers as Emile Durkheim, Karl Marx, Max Scheler, Georg Simmel, and Max Weber and later by social investigators such as Deutsch (1973), Festinger (1954), Frank (1967), Fromm (1973), Goffman (1963), Lewin (1948), Parsons (1967), and Sherif and Sherif (1969). They described various aspects of the social psychology of intergroup conflicts, including the six major ones summarized by Taylor and Moghaddam (1987), each of which explains the source of the conflict differently:

1.   realistic conflict

2.   social identity

3.   equity

4.   relative deprivation

5.   elite

6.   the five-stage model.

Moreover, the specialized literature on conflict resolution is full of models and strategies for turning conflict into cooperation and bringing peace to relationships of all kinds, if both opponents would only do what is suggested (Bisno 1988; Bloomfield and Moulton 1997; Cornelius and Faire 1989; Crum 1976; Curle 1971; Donahue and Kolt 1993; Filley 1975; Fisher and Brown 1988; Fisher and Ury 1981; Galtung 1996; Mindell 1995; Pruitt and Rubin 1986; Rose 1998; Rosenberg 2000; Rothman 1992; Rummel 1975–1981; Sharp 1973, 2005; Slaikeu 1996; Walters 1981; Walton 1969; Woodhouse 1991).

Application of psychological knowledge in the pursuit of peace

Some of these interdisciplinary professionals were involved in various attempts to create a new profession of applied social scientists to advise national policy makers on conflict resolution and war prevention. This profession would look at major cultural, political, and social events through the prism of social psychology and psychiatry. One of the earliest attempts by mental health professionals to influence politicians was carried out by a committee on war "prophylaxis" initiated by the Netherlands Medical Society (1939) a few years before the Second World War. They sent the following open letter to government officials, newspapers, and private individuals all over the world:

> It seems to us that there is in the world a mentality, which entails grave dangers to mankind, leading as it may, to an evident war-psychosis. War means that all destructive forces are set loose by mankind against itself. War means the annihilation of mankind by technical science. As in all things human, psychological factors play a very important part in the complicated problem of war. If war is to be prevented the nations and their leaders must understand their own attitude toward war. By self-knowledge a world calamity may be prevented...we come to you with the urgent advice to arouse the nations to the realization of the fact and the sense of collective self-preservation, these powerful instincts being the strongest allies for the elimination of war.

Three hundred and thirty-nine psychiatrists from 30 countries signed the letter; and although they received many encouraging responses, unsurprisingly, Germany, Italy, and Japan were not among them.

The devastating consequences of the Second World War confirmed the warnings of this committee but did not deter other psychiatrists from attempting to prevent further violence. Indeed, in 1945, Flugel suggested we look upon war as a kind of mass delinquency. He postulated that, if psychology could be of use in dealing with an individual's misdemeanors, it might also be helpful in dealing with the more grandiose immoralities of nations. As a result, the main effort during these postwar years was to understand the behavior of Nazi mass murderers, explaining their behavior with psychological theories. Some of the famous anti-Semites were analyzed, categorized, and diagnosed as suffering from some type of mental illness or criminal predisposition; but because these Nazis turned out to be such complicated cases, being both loving parents and cruel murderers at the same time, they kept institutions full of psychoanalysts happily engaged in contradictory arguments for years without any clear-cut explanations.

From a different scientific perspective, a group of professionals in the early 1950s tried to develop a general theory of human conflict based on game theory (Axelrod 1984), decision theory, and statistical modeling. However, according to Harty and Modell (1991), these attempts were largely unsuccessful.

During the protests against the Vietnam War in the 1960s and early 1970s, many psychologists from the field of humanistic psychology became involved in international peace promotion. One of the most inspired proponents of this approach was the American psychologist Carl Rogers (1965). He asked mental health professionals to use encounter group principles to help solve conflicts on a global scale, whether interpersonal, marital, interracial, intergroup, or international. Rogers was followed by a group of humanistic psychologists who also believed that therapy groups could be employed as holistic-political tools to make peace between the United States and the USSR and to promote a communion of brotherhood between all human beings. Along the same lines and within the same humanistic movement, Maslow (1977) suggested that:

> any method is good that fosters communication, understanding, intimacy, trust, openness, honesty, self-exposure, feedback, awareness, compassion, tolerance, acceptance, friendliness, love, and that reduces suspicion, paranoid expectations, fear, feelings of being different, enmity, defensiveness, envy, contempt, insult, condescension, polarization, splitting, alienation, and separation. (p.16)

This field has become even more popular during the last few decades and is still in vogue. In this present time of global terrorism (Covington *et al.* 2002), mental health professionals try to explain what makes a "terrorist tick." As a result, there are now many organizations trying to apply psychological knowledge in the pursuit of peace. There are also various interdisciplinary professional journals devoted to this issue, such as the journal *Political Behavior*. This journal publishes original research in the general fields of political behavior, broadly construed to include institutions, processes, and policies as well as individual political behavior.

Presently, one of the foremost psychoanalysts of political situations is Vamik Volkan, a professor of psychiatry at the University of Virginia. He uses his understanding as a consultant in conflict negotiation and resolution in a great variety of intergroup conflicts around the world. Among his contributions, his understanding of large-group identities (i.e. ethnic, national, religious, ideological) allows the practitioner to examine societal processes through a psychoanalytic lens and to suggest ways in which such processes become less malignant. Together with colleagues from the Center for the Study of Mind and Human Interaction, Volkan (1999) developed an interdisciplinary methodology for reducing ethnic tensions between opposing large groups. This approach promotes peaceful and adaptive coexistence, integration, or absorption. Nicknamed the "tree model" to reflect the slow unfolding of the process like the slow growth and branching of a tree, it has three basic components or phases:

1.   Psychopolitical diagnosis of the situation includes in-depth interviews with a wide range of members of the groups involved. The interdisciplinary team of clinicians, historians, political scientists, and others map out the main aspects of the relationship between the two groups and the situation to be addressed.

2.   Psychopolitical dialogues between members of opposing groups consist of a series of multiday meetings over several years. In such meetings, resistances are brought to the surface, articulated, and interpreted so that more realistic communication can take place.

3.   Collaborative actions and institutions that grow out of the dialogue process pertain to the translation of insights into actual social and political policy, as well as into actions and programs that have concrete effects upon the populations.

Early efforts to find psychological solutions to the problem of war were in some ways affiliated with religious and spiritual approaches to conflict resolution, such as those proposed by Mahatma Gandhi, the Dalai Lama, and Martin Luther King, Jr. First, Mahatma Gandhi's philosophy of nonviolence was universally adopted. Second, the recommendation of the fourteenth and current Dalai Lama of Tibetan Buddhism to resolve disagreements through dialogue was widely accepted. Finally, the influence of Rev. Dr Martin Luther King, Jr was pivotal to this peace movement. In a Christmas sermon on peace, delivered on December 24 1967 at Ebenezer Baptist Church in Atlanta, Georgia, he said:

> Now let me suggest first that if we are to have peace on earth, our loyalties must become ecumenical rather than sectional. Our loyalties must transcend our race, our tribe, our class, and our nation; and this means we must develop a world perspective. No individual can live alone; no nation can live alone, and as long as we try, the more we are going to have war in this world. Now the judgment of God is upon us,

and we must either learn to live together as brothers or we are all going to perish together as fools. (King 1967)

Brotherly love, however, is difficult to ask of people who are unjustly attacked by hostile forces.

While Gandhi's principles of *ahimsa* (nonviolence) might have worked well in the fight against the British, they did not stop the escalating tensions between Hindus and Muslims in India. Many believe that Gandhi's nonviolence failed because he was dismayed by the treatment of the Muslim minority in India by Hinduism and by the resulting calls for the creation of a separate Muslim state, Pakistan. Widespread distrust and hatred grew between Hindus and Muslims and, on the eve of India's independence, riots erupted all over India. The country became a bloodbath in which an estimated one million lives were lost (Wolpert 1991).

Such religious riots still erupt on a regular basis, despite the nonviolent influence of Gandhi. For example, in 2002, in Ahmedabad, India (the adopted hometown of Gandhi), Hindu mobs committed acts of unspeakable savagery against Muslims. The violence raged for days and persisted for more than two months, claiming almost 1000 lives. It was driven by hatred and sparked by a terrible crime: a Muslim mob stoned a train car loaded with activists from the World Hindu Council and then set it on fire, killing 59 people, mostly women and children. The day after the train attack, police officers arrested not a single person from among the tens of thousands rampaging through Muslim enclaves.

Though many of the above-mentioned peace activists and humanistic psychologists might have been correct from a psychological point of view, intergroup conflicts are surely more complex and more resistant to change than these professionals had assumed. Not only did they fail to recognize that some tensions are grounded in real and substantial disputes, but they also did not differentiate between the emotional, intrapsychic, interpersonal, and group-as-a-whole sources of conflicts that demand integrative approaches to conflict transformation rather than one-sided encounter approaches.

Primary aggression

Most obviously missing were their refusal to acknowledge any primary hostile or evil human inclination as a source of conflict (Adams 1989; Staub 1989) and their almost passionate rejection of Freud's (1930) assertion that aggression may be instinctual rather than a response to frustration (Okey

1992). As a result, their approaches to conflict resolution lacked realistic appraisals of the possible multidetermination of human aggression, including instinct, drive, genetic makeup, environmental provocation, and social situation (Bandura 1973), and the need therefore to deal with conflict in a variety of ways.

Contrary to these humanistic psychologists, I believe any sound approach to sociodramatic conflict transformation must take into account the possibility that Freud was correct in his critique of the "love thy neighbor" principle, because:

> men are not gentle creatures who want to be loved...they are on the contrary, creatures among whose instinctual endowments is to be reckoned a powerful share of aggressiveness. As a result, their neighbor is for them...someone to cause him pain, to torture and to kill him... Who, in the face of all his experience of life and history, will have the courage to dispute this assertion? (1930, p.111–112)

Einstein was similarly occupied with this question when he asked Freud if hatred and destruction satisfy an innate human drive, which ordinarily remains latent but which can easily be aroused and intensified to the point of mass psychosis. Freud's long response can be simplified in a short sentence: people are aggressive creatures by nature and they therefore need to be restrained either by themselves from the inside or by society from the outside. As a result of such innate aggression, Freud warned that, if the very thin layer of human culture and civilization broke, groups would clash like primal hordes. On the basis of this rationale, Freud (1930) went on to say, "It is always possible to bind together a considerable number of people in love, so long as there are other people left over to receive the manifestations of their aggressiveness" (p.114).

Unfortunately, Freud's observations seem to remain valid. History has taught that there are cruel people who want nothing else but to cause death and destruction. We may even assume that there is a kind of blind and senseless hatred in certain people, which I have called "unconditional hate" (Halasz and Kellermann 2005; Kellermann 2005), as a direct opposite of unconditional love. People should be justified in defending themselves against such hate, even with violent means. In such circumstances, war in itself cannot be seen as inherently unethical. If a people or a country is resisting such aggression, defending itself from any external attack or from violations of its basic rights, its armed forces can be characterized as waging a "just war" (Johnson 1981, 1987).

Though space does not permit a full discussion of Freud's theories on the primacy of human aggression nor of the various violent and nonviolent means of defense, I do believe it is important to take a firm position on this issue when working with sociodramatic conflict resolution. I have, therefore, added an emotional dimension to the conflict model presented here.

Moreover, from a sociological point of view, I believe sociodrama should be firmly grounded in a theory of social conflict or consensus. According to the functionalist theories of Parsons (1967) and Merton (1968), social balance (and love) is an ideal virtue. However, social discord is a natural part of the conflict theory of Karl Marx. What's more, cooperation and conflict (love and hate) coexist in society, according to Lensky (1966); so some conflicts may be highly desirable, adding some spice to living that provides incentives to achieve personal or group goals. Through cooperation, people may see their differences as assets, enriching the group and allowing it to succeed. Differences between people are thus appreciated because they add valuable resources to the group as a whole. In contrast, destructive conflicts are based on a competitive worldview in which only one person can win while the other must lose (Deutsch 1973). Any attempt to suggest a viable conflict-resolution strategy must take such basic views of people and society and cooperation and competition into consideration.

Interpersonal conflicts are universally present in human relations and become especially visible in all group activity. The mere fact of being together in a group assures that there will always be some amount of friction among its members. Though such frictions may have apparent negative effects on the group, they are not necessarily something bad or pathological to be removed. Rather, like states of crises, conflicts may be viewed as normal in healthy relations and, if properly managed, as opportunities for development, growth, and new learning (Bach and Goldberg 1974; Cornelius and Faire 1989; Gans 1989; Ormont 1984). Concerning this issue, we are guided by Pines' (1988) recommendation that "group analysts are trained to be sensitive to the balance between cooperation and conflict in the groups...[and] they bring to the attention of the group members the presence of both these centripetal and centrifugal forces" (p.57).

In view of the social and political tensions in many countries, the distinctions between constructive and destructive conflicts in the development, maintenance, and resolution of conflict have been increasingly blurred. Some practitioners respond with bewildered confusion and helplessness when called upon to manage situations in which people are openly antagonistic towards one another, either passively waiting for the tensions to diminish by themselves or observing how they develop into a general feeling of alienation, which threatens to tear the group apart. Others employ resolution techniques in an orthodox and automatic fashion, without sufficient consideration as to what the fight is all about from the various points of view represented. As a result, conflicts essential for the exploratory and therapeutic process of the group remain insufficiently explored during the course of therapy.

Drawing on interviews with several group therapists, on surveys of the literature (Bisno 1988; Cowger 1979; Deutsch 1973; Donahue and Kolt 1993; Doob 1985; Fisher and Ury 1981; Walton 1969), and on conclusions from my own experience, I here describe four strategies of conflict transformation and discuss some of the controversies involved in their use within sociodrama.

Conflict transformation

Considering the complex and almost infinite sources of conflicts, management is surely a formidable undertaking. Obviously, transformation approaches may be chosen according to what the fight is all about. There is a continuum of emotional, intrapsychic, interactional, and group-related variables at work in any conflict. The sociodramatist must choose to focus on one or all of these, choosing to intervene on the various emotional, individual, interpersonal, and social levels in succession and combination if multiple sources of conflict are revealed.

For example, if suppression of aggression seems to be the underlying cause of tension, the sociodramatist may focus first on the emotional expression of aggression and suggest the opponents honestly "talk it out" or find a way to fight or compete that gets rid of the frustration while not causing physical harm to anyone. If transference-related issues later become predominant, the individual approach, which emphasizes intrapsychic transformation, may be employed. The interpersonal approach with the sociodramatist acting as mediator or facilitator of communication may be chosen when interactional disturbances are observed. Finally, when global group dynamic factors seem to have caused the conflict, an analysis of the meaning of the conflict for the group as a whole may be considered.

Table 7.1 gives an overview of these four overlapping and highly interrelated approaches, their theoretical bases, and their main objectives. Together, they constitute a general model of conflict transformation, which can be integratively used in succession or combination during the various phases of the transformation process.

Table 7.1 Model of conflict transformation approaches

Approaches	Theoretical basis	Main objective
Emotional	Frustration–aggression	Expression of pent-up aggression
Intrapsychic	Transference displacement	Correction of perceptual distortion
Interpersonal	Interaction	Improved communication
Group-as-a-whole	Social psychology of groups	Transformation of group dynamics

The leader may simply and succinctly interpret these four conflict transformation approaches in the following manner:

1. You are angry because you are full of frustration! If each one of you expresses aggressions and gets them out of your bodies, you may be able to get along together better.

2. You are angry at one another because you can't stand him and you can't stand her. Both of you need to take responsibility for your own anger, which says more about you than about the other person. If you realize that he is not all you want him to be and she is not all you want her to be, you may be able to accept one another as you really are and get along together better.

3. You are angry at one another because you don't get along well together. The problem lies not within either one of you but in the special interaction, or complementarity, between both of you. If both learn how to give and take collectively, you may be able to cooperate better.

4. You are angry at one another because of "them," because you exist in a context that puts you in a position of conflict. If you learn to

recognize and separate this outside pressure from your relationship and unite to cope with it, you may be able to get along together better.

I believe these four approaches to interpersonal conflict transformation are all-inclusive and sum it all up.

The emotional approach

According to the emotional approach, aggression is primary and instinctive, almost like the aggression in animals. Such aggression is motivated by either territorial defense, predatory aggression, inter-male aggression, fear-induced aggression (preceded by attempts to escape), irritable aggression evoked by any attackable object or other animal, maternal (protective) aggression, or instrumental aggression (Moyer 1968). It is used for self-defense, competition (social conflict), predation, and protection of our offspring (Brain 1979). As emphasized by Scheff (1994), war is also instigated on the basis of national-ism and bloody revenge.

Depending on the environmental circumstances and the functionality of the behavior, the similarities of animal aggressive behavior to that of humans are obvious. In humans, we often describe such aggression as "primitive," a primordial tendency to safeguard the continuation of one's biological existence or, like a "holy war," something that transcends any logic or reason. When functioning at such primitive levels of behavior, people become uncivi-lized and selfish, taking what they need without thinking about the conse-quences. Though it is clearly antisocial, such nonrational behavior cannot be subject to moral judgment and cannot be depicted as "evil" because it is fully utilitarian and driven by physiological needs. Whatever "hate" may be present is easily understood as the expression of the basic fear of losing something that is inherently needed.

To make participants aware of such emotions, the sociodramatist may invite a group to enact a situation that contains a demarcation between two parties or countries living side by side. There is a common border between them, which sometimes is a river or an open field. This middle land is a "no man's" land. On both sides, people of different cultures live with little or no contact with the other side. Sometimes, there is a bridge over the river but not always. Participants take one or the other side and improvise an interaction between them. This role-playing exercise may contain a conflict element, such as the presence of some valued material on one side or a land dispute, or may simply focus on the different needs of each side. After the action, group members share their experiences, discussing what they have learned from the exercise in terms of the kinds of feelings evoked at various points of the drama.

Such an exercise quickly makes it clear there are no simple solutions to border disputes. Indeed, according to Galtung (1996), war will erupt whenever one of more than 2000 *nations* (which are bound together by culture, religion, and history) competes for any of the only 200 *states* (geographically defined territories or countries) available. Simply put, groups of people want to be ruled over not by others, but by their own people.

According to Flugel (1945), war may bring:

- adventure (the lure of the unknown, new opportunities, sacrifice, or asceticism)
- cohesion (bringing the nation together in shared interest and social unity)
- relief (from individual worries and restrictions, with social concerns taking precedence)
- a socially accepted outlet for people's aggression.

All these reasons for going to war are in addition to the greed and hubris of many leaders of states.

Whatever reason is given, we can expect two human groups that compete for territorial power, perceived as necessary for their own self-preservation, will go to war with great determination. Ever since Cain and Abel, such wars have been passionate enterprises; people have attacked one another and have murdered, butchered, and assaulted one another by the thousands because of such competition. On each side, warriors with a well-developed killer instinct have practiced their skills without guilt or remorse, and they have been generously rewarded and glorified for their services by their own people. Because of the competition for territorial power, these wars have been perceived as just and the conflicts based on realistic reasons.

Although such a primitive point of view concerning conflicts may seem repulsive to peace-loving people today, it must be considered in any conflict transformation approach. Sociodramatists working according to this emotional approach attempt to resolve conflicts primarily by encouraging people to unload whatever pent-up anger they may have been keeping in. The main assumption underlying this approach is the well-known frustration–aggression theory of Dollard *et al.* (1939), later reformulated by Berkowitz (1989). According to this view, any frustration or interference with a person's goal-directed activities causes the person to react with aggression that, whether innate or reactive (Simmel, Hahn and Walters 1983), must somehow find expression. If sufficient outlet is denied, the aggression builds like steam in a pressure cooker, bursting to relieve the pressure and causing a variety of emotional and physical disturbances (Rubin 1969; Smith 1992).

The best way to get rid of this aggression is to let it out through some overt expression. This need not be a violent confrontation, however, as such aggression may be channeled through vicarious cathartic experiences. Among the socially accepted outlets for such emotions are those encouraged and permitted within international competitive sports tournaments.

Sociodrama may also be a safe and suitable place for such vicariously aggressive activity: a kind of laboratory for learning how to express anger towards other people. In such an expressive approach, participants are encouraged to express their present anger in an honest, direct manner rather than with the tact and restraint characteristic of people's behavior in ordinary social situations. In action-oriented forms of group therapy, such as encounter groups, bioenergetics, Gestalt, and psychodrama, and in marathon, sensitivity, and human potential growth groups, participants are urged to express their anger both in words and in action; they are encouraged to scream, bang on an empty chair, stamp on the floor, or throw objects at the wall, simultaneously pronouncing their outrage verbally. Frequently, mattresses, pillows, or *batacas* (foam rubber bats) are used for pounding; and two people involved in a fight may be urged to push each other down or wrestle in any manner they wish (as long as nobody gets hurt).

While such an active approach would be unacceptable within a psychoanalytic framework of nonstructured verbal interaction, the focus on emotional expression per se, as manifested in the interpretation of various defenses (Rutan, Alonso and Groves 1988), is also emphasized in verbal group therapies. Expressing anger directly towards other people is also a part of all behavioral assertiveness training in which participants are taught to behave assertively rather than submissively in interpersonal conflicts. First, they become more in touch with the physical manifestations of their anger. Second, they accept anger as a legitimate emotion even though they may wish to be without it. Third, they explore the precipitating frustrations and identify the possible sources of anger. Fourth, they try out nonverbal as well as verbal ways of expressing anger (i.e. through body posture, tone of voice, and eye contact). In this process, feelings previously denied expression are let out as fully as possible. Finally, participants try out their newly learned behaviors in situations outside the therapy setting.

The notion that expression leads to relief is easily accepted. Such release helps break the vicious circle of frustration–aggression–inhibition–repression, which so often characterizes neurotic people. Yet the question of whether or not such an emotional approach can resolve conflicts remains. Critics (e.g. Tavris 1983) hold that aggressive expression not only is a worthless way of resolving conflicts but actually makes people angrier than before. Similarly, with a mass of accumulated evidence from research studies on children, Bandura and Walters (1965) concluded that, far from producing reduction of aggression, participation in aggressive behavior maintains the behavior at its original level or actually increases it.

The personalities of the people involved must also be considered. While expression may clearly provide a safety valve for surplus anger for people emotionally restricted and inhibited and for compulsive personalities excessively concerned with conformity and adherence to standards of conscience, impulsive personalities who have explosive outbursts of aggression need to develop internal controls to restrain their overt anger and may be less suited to this approach.

Furthermore, the effect of expression seems to be highly influenced by the responses people receive to their overt aggression. When the expression of anger is met with retaliation, the experience usually results in new frustration, not relief. The new experience becomes reconciliatory and perhaps corrective only when the expression is accepted and the antagonist openly admits to being wrong. Thus, giving expression to anger heretofore kept in can be an important learning experience that paves the way for other more cognitive and interpersonal approaches to conflict transformation.

The intrapsychic approach

According to the intrapsychic approach, conflicts are based on our tendency to view other people with bitterness, distrust, or resentment. The main assumption underlying this approach is that people reject one another because of their negative subjective evaluations of the other. Women may, for example, say to men, "We don't like you because you're so selfish!" The intrapsychic approach does not focus on the selfishness of men in this case but on the perception of the women. Clearly, the men do not live up to the expectations of the women, the women need to be more appreciated, the women feel neglected, etc.

In international relations, derogatory evaluations of others are common and may lead to violent eruptions of conflict. As exemplified by Volkan (1988), Al Qaeda terrorist groups view all Americans as demons and infidels to be annihilated, and many Americans view bearded Muslims in a similar manner. Many Israelis consider Palestinians subhuman, and most Palestinians think Israelis are despoilers of the land they are supposed to share. Such division of groups into "us" and "them" has been described in detail by social identity theory (Tajfel 1981), which is very relevant to the intrapsychic approach. When states are divided along ethnic, linguistic, or tribal lines, any mass paranoia plays into the hands of politicians who want to be reelected (Robins and Post 1997) because blaming everything on an outside enemy strengthens the inner unity of any country. Intragroup tension almost ceases to exist because all aggression is directed outwards towards the other group.

In his book *Bloodlines: from ethnic pride to ethnic terrorism*, Volkan (1997) suggested that people kill one another for the sake of protecting and maintaining their own large-group identities. The group's "we-ness" becomes so deadly that it feels compelled to take revenge for wrongs inflicted on its ancestors or others belonging to its bloodline. Hundreds of years of tribal mentality and of men sacrificing their lives for their countries contribute to this situation.

Some of this division of "we" and "them," however, is clearly based on perceptual distortions of the other group. These sometimes become clear through the use of the psychodramatic mirror technique. We become aware of hating the other person because there is something in that individual that is part of ourselves and we become highly disturbed to see it so clearly in the other person.

In chapter 6, we described the tendencies of one group to view the other through its own ethnocentric prism. We have also observed that projecting negative images upon other people increases when the groups come into close proximity. Practitioners working according to this intrapsychic approach attempt to resolve conflicts primarily by focusing on the hostility experienced by either one or both of the conflicting parties and interpreting such hostilities as expressions of their subjective perceptions.

Confronting individuals with their highly subjective ways of relating to each other may create the basis for more realistic relations. People may get to know the other persons in new and more positive lights. By changing the focus from the antagonist to themselves, they become more aware of the role the antagonist serves as a repository of disowned parts of themselves (Pines 1988). This can often be traced first to similar roles in their present social network and later to the same roles within the family of origin. Frequently, conflicts may be resolved by either party becoming aware of the blame it places on the other for not fulfilling uncompleted quests from the past. Depending on the training of the sociodramatist, all of this work may be done more or less in action.

While group psychotherapists of all persuasions use the intrapsychic approach frequently, its effectiveness as a conflict resolution technique is arguable. Critics hold that it cannot resolve interpersonal conflicts because, by emphasizing the intrapsychic source of hostility, the possible real evil nature of other people is insufficiently recognized. Instead of directing one's anger towards the other person, one is urged to look into oneself and, as a result, one may blame oneself for wrongdoings that one did not commit.

Thus, legitimate aggression may be inhibited, introjected, or sublimated instead of directed towards the person originally responsible for the frustration. Advocates find this critique oversimplified and dismissive as it does not take into account the interactive perspective of the object-relations model, which focuses on how one person's intrapsychic state of mind affects another's. Therefore, when the dynamics of both "projectors" and "targets" are analyzed within the same exchange, the intrapsychic approach becomes profoundly effective.

However, interpersonal conflict is rarely a case of one person being completely at fault and the other totally innocent. More typically, "it takes two to start a fight." Consequently, practitioners should focus on the interaction between both parties in the dispute, not just on the intrapsychic world within each person.

The interpersonal approach

The main assumption underlying the interpersonal approach is that conflicts typically occur in a social context involving at least two persons who, for various reasons, do not get along. For example, we tend to dislike people who are different from us in values and beliefs; who do not reciprocate our liking for them; and who are abusive, malicious, and generally unfriendly towards us. The correlation between attraction and similarity is robustly described in the social psychological literature. Various theories, such as transaction theory, reinforcement theory (Byrne and Clore 1970), and exchange theory (Homans 1961), emphasize that, if there is insufficient mutuality, interdependency, balance, and complementarity between the parties involved in a relationship, interpersonal conflicts will arise. Complementarity (Carson 1969) refers to reciprocity and correspondence on the power-status or affiliation dimensions (Leary 1957) and to symmetrical interactions on the control or equality dimensions (Bateson 1979).

Violent conflicts between believers of various religious and sectarian per-suasions have always existed. Examples abound. Hindu–Muslim coexistence is almost inconceivable. Everything pulls them apart. They not only look at the world differently but also have different concepts of society and opposing ideals of equality and hierarchical systems. As a result, there is much distrust, devaluation, and fear between them that, after the British withdrawal, have led to continual wars between India and Pakistan (1947–1949, 1965, and 1971). The same is true for the two major Islamic sects in Iraq: Sunni and Shiite. Though the two groups are very similar, they have sharp political dif-ferences. Among Christians, disagreements between the Ukrainian Orthodox, Russian Orthodox, Greek Catholic, and Roman Catholic churches have continued for centuries. In addition, all of these have strained relations with Protestant churches. Religious dogma has always played a role in such conflicts, and the centuries-old enmity between the three Abrahamitic religions – Judaism, Christianity, and Islam – is as vibrant as ever. Finally, there are frequent skirmishes between Muslims and Christians in Nigeria. A recent religious riot began when Muslims in the north demonstrated against cartoons satirizing the Prophet Muhammad. More than 30 Christians were killed in riots in two mainly Muslim towns. Thereafter, crowds of Christians armed with machetes killed more than 80 people in Onitsha during two days of reprisal attacks.

Instead of compatibility and cooperation, such interpersonal conflicts are characterized by tension and friction and by competition, jealousy, or power struggles in which both parties feel "I am right and you are wrong" or "I am good and you are bad." Invariably, poor communication is a common ingredi-ent. The head-on collision between two sets of irreconcilable beliefs creates interpersonal conflict (Rogers 1965).

Such conflicts escalate as long as the parties continue to provoke one another; in some cases, they end only in final, violent confrontations. As described in game theory (Luce and Raiffa 1957), people in conflict play a competitive game with one another, as in the classic duel of two men walking towards each other with guns leveled, the outcome being that one will win and the other will lose. Bloomfield and Leiss (1969) and Bloomfield and Moulton (1997) described the gradual escalation of the intensity of a conflict. Starting with a minor dispute or simple quarrel, it escalates into a conflict with military options, finally reaching open hostility involving combat between organized military forces. The development of each phase is influenced by events and conditions, which either generate pressures moving the situation toward increased violence (or its threat) or provide some resolution and move the situation away from violence.

To settle such fights in a way different from the destructive win/lose scenario, practitioners attempt to mediate between the parties, trying to make peace between them. Mediation occurs whenever an impartial third party attempts to facilitate a voluntary agreement between two or more parties in conflict (Folberg and Taylor 1984; Walton 1969). Psychoanalytic group leaders take the roles of mediators when they act as interpreters and catalysts of the interaction, attempting to facilitate communication to modify the inter-action pattern and improve understanding between the conflicting parties by recognizing the subtle transactional configurations and feedback mechanisms that support both the adult and childish elements in the relationship (Rapoport 1988). More behaviorally oriented group leaders mediate by giving advice; teaching fair play; and using logic, diplomacy, and emotional appeasement to help disputants reach mutually acceptable solutions.

Successful mediation, however, does not necessarily imply mutual consensus. According to Blood (1960), other possible satisfactory outcomes of mediation may be:

- compromise – both go half way and get some of their demands satisfied

- concession – one side drops its demands and is allowed a graceful retreat

- synthesis – a new solution is found that was hitherto not considered

- separation – both go their own ways

- accommodation, essentially a kind of resignation and recognition of failing to reach agreement – both agree to disagree.

Likewise, in marital therapy, couples in conflict may achieve a higher level of agreement, whether the outcome is staying married or obtaining a divorce (Sholevar 1981).

Maxwell Jones's charismatic leadership style (Ascher and Shokol 1976) presents another creative mediation strategy for conflicts that evolve within therapeutic communities. Jones resolved conflicts through subtle redefinitions of clashes between people – "troublemakers" became "risk-takers," "power struggles" became "shared decision making," "conflict" became "confrontation" – and thus he succeeded in transforming potentially negative and destructive interpersonal tensions into positive learning opportunities. Educators and organizational consultants in institutions all over the world use many such subtle methods of reframing.

The relevant literature is full of accounts of nonviolent resolutions of a variety of conflicts resulting from successful mediation by third parties (e.g. Fisher 1983; Rubin 1980). However, textbooks on the subject (e.g. Deutsch 1973) emphasize that, if the initial positions of the conflicting parties are compatible and the relationship is based on cooperation and trust, the interpersonal approach will be more effective than if the initial attitudes are incompatible and the relationship is based on rivalry and competition. If the parties have something to gain from remaining involved in a power struggle, mediation will surely fail.

Reciprocal role reversal

The most common action-oriented mediation technique frequently recommended for conflict transformation within sociodrama is reciprocal role reversal. This technique, borrowed from psychodrama, is based on the assumption that, if antagonists put themselves in the position of the other, they will be forced to take a new view of the situation and reconcile their differences (Kellermann 1992).

If a protagonist and an antagonist are involved in an interpersonal conflict, in the first phase, both clarify their positions. Then, they are asked to reverse roles, the protagonist becoming the antagonist and the antagonist, the protagonist. In their new roles, they are asked to repeat the other person's position. They are again asked to return to their own original positions and each gets an opportunity to respond. If necessary, such role reversals continue as long as needed to clarify all the pros and cons of the situation. When this has been done to the satisfaction of both parties, they are both asked to step out of the situation and watch themselves from outside, as if in a mirror. Two other group members play both roles and summarize the basic arguments. The two original parties comment on what they see from this outside and impartial position. They are then asked for a possible solution to the problem. Each one has a chance to come up with a creative solution that makes every effort to take into consideration both points of view.

Role reversal demands from the antagonists an immediate shift in positions, aimed at facilitating some kind of mutual understanding and reconciliation. Obviously, however, reciprocal role reversal does not automatically produce a change of mind in any of the conflicting parties. Unfortunately, positive outcomes of reciprocal role reversals in interpersonal and intergroup conflicts are rare and reconciliation is usually hard to achieve. It has been my experience that two people involved in a head-on collision are stubbornly unwilling to reverse roles truly with one another as long as they perceive the other person as an enemy. If they do agree to reverse roles, they do so for a short period of time, repeating the main message of their opponent and then resorting to their old position of "I am right and you are wrong."

This technique will cause individuals holding opposing attitudes to come closer together only if their initial positions are compatible. However, if their initial attitudes are incompatible, the parties will move further apart (Johnson and Dustin 1970, p.149). Thus, while we still know too little about the effects of reciprocal role reversal to recommend the blind use of it in all conflict situations, it is likely that reciprocal role reversal will be more effective in cooperative relations than in competitive ones. However, even if no solution is found, the technique may create a more positive atmosphere, reflecting the search for a solution to end the conflict rather than only trying to win the battle and thus escalating the tension.

The use of role reversal with oppressed and traumatized people further complicates its use in all situations of conflict. As pointed out by Ochberg (1988), victims of violence are very sensitive to being blamed for the wrong done to them. Therefore, as a general rule, protagonists who have been hurt by other people should not be asked to reverse roles with these same people. They first need to become more in touch with their own feelings of anger, which are so often confused and chaotic. Most importantly, their pent-up aggression needs first to be asserted and channeled to the outside source of aggression before an understanding of the other people's position may be encouraged. Any premature request for role reversal at this stage runs the risk of being interpreted by protagonists as a subtle message to understand the motives of the others and to accept the injustice that was done to them. As a result, they may turn their aggression against themselves and feel guilty or further repress their true selves. Reciprocal role reversal for reconciliation may be suggested only in those cases in which the victims themselves, often after a long process of trauma resolution, express a need to take the role of the other.

In addition to these precautionary observations, Carlson-Sabelli (1989) did not find sufficient research evidence to verify the assumption that role reversal actually does promote reconciliation between parties in conflict. Possibly, there needs to be a prior period of hostile ventilation and intrapsychic exploration to make the antagonists really willing to listen to the position of the other. Consequently, Moreno's vision that lasting peace between people and nations will be achieved if the capacity to reverse roles is only cultivated must be considered naive and utopian.

Though interpersonal learning is regarded as one of the most powerful therapeutic aspects in group psychotherapy (Yalom 1975), many practitioners feel personally uncomfortable with the mediation role of the interpersonal approach; they do not want to act as peace-makers who implicitly promote norms of friendly coexistence and reconciliation at the expense of natural human aggression. Rather, they prefer that the group members decide for themselves which norms they want to adopt regarding the boundaries of hostile expression. As a result, many group leaders prefer to shift the focus of intervention from the parties involved in the conflict to the group as a whole.

The group-as-a-whole approach

Group leaders who work according to the group-as-a-whole approach (e.g. Foulkes 1964; Kibel and Stein 1981) take into account the whole context in which conflicts occur and apply concepts of individual dynamics to the group as if the group were able to behave, feel, and think like an individual. They view intragroup tensions as a specific disharmony in the structure or general system (Durkin 1972) of the entire group, considering also the effects on the group of the larger environment and ecology. In addition, social psychology has contributed much to our understanding of how social forces in the group as a whole disturb the interpersonal relations between individual members of a group (Cartwright and Zander 1968; Shaw 1976; Sherif and Sherif 1969). According to Hoffman (2002):

> Many studies in the field of conflict resolution show that some conflicts are caused not by the people involved but by the system or social

structure within which they are obliged to operate. Even if you were to insert two saints into such a system the saints would soon end up in conflict with each other.

When investigating such social forces, small-group research has for decades tried to describe the intricate relationship between conflict and the group setting, group composition, group size, group norms, group process, leadership roles, and stages in the development of groups, assuming that aggression is a regulating force in the dynamics of groups. Within his field theory, Kurt Lewin (1948) drew together insights from topology (e.g. life space), psychology (e.g. need, aspiration, etc.), and sociology (e.g. force fields) to explain how various forces can both facilitate and prevent change in large groups. For change to take place, Lewin (1951) believed the total situation (field or matrix) has to be taken into account. This total situation is the social environment, which works as a dynamic field that constantly interacts with human consciousness, and also the whole psychological field, or the "life space," which includes the family, workplace, school, and church. Thus, person and environment are mutually interdependent. If the social environment is adjusted, there immediately follows a new feeling in the members. In turn, if individual members are more satisfied, there is more harmony in the society.

Lewin's theory was succinctly illustrated in the movie *Star Wars* when Luke Skywalker says "May the force be with you!" indicating there is something larger that is influencing everything, something like a supernatural force or strong energy field that is at work and can be restrained with great effort. To paraphrase Skywalker within the present group-as-a-whole approach to sociodramatic conflict resolution, we would greet individuals and groups with the blessing "May the society be with you!"

When managing conflicts according to this approach, the task of the sociodramatist is to analyze and handle these various social forces and transform those that have a restrictive effect on the group into more enabling ones. To achieve this goal, practitioners of various persuasions employ more or less interpretative or action-oriented techniques to facilitate cooperation and the development of group cohesion, the "prime prerequisite for the successful management of conflict" (Yalom 1975, p.355). In this process, joint interest in the goals of the group is fostered and active participation by all group members is encouraged. The sociodramatist makes a democratic effort to involve the resources and reactions of the noncombatant members of the group, inviting them to contribute, resonate, or help resolve emergent issues regarding concerns such as confidentiality, decision making, and social interaction outside the group.

For example, when there is tension between various religious communities, as expressed in acts of violence against one or the other religious institution, representatives may be invited from the various groups to a common meeting to discuss common policy of religious freedom. In parts of Europe and the US, such interreligious meetings between Protestant, Catholic, and Jewish congregations have led to better understanding and coexistence between local groups in multicultural communities. At one such meeting, the solution not only concerned religious practices but also dealt with the problems found in providing better housing, enhancing transportation, and building recreational facilities for the youth in the area. Such places allowed members of different backgrounds to meet on a regular basis and to cooperate in sports, cultural, and community events. Although there may be little attitude change resulting from such meetings, there will be less open violence and more opportunities to settle disputes before they escalate into street riots and open warfare.

Most group analysts adopt a neutral position towards the group, observing and reporting on group conflict without siding for or against any of the parties involved. Critics (e.g. Bach 1974) hold that such an attitude of objective passivity violates the intimate spirit of authentic interpersonal relations and makes any effort toward genuine conflict transformation impossible. They argue that such a laissez-faire attitude (disguised as neutrality) is as useless as United Nations troops who leave the field of battle when the fighting starts. It is my position that sociodramatists who have an interest in conflict transformation must occasionally take firm and positive stands on crucial issues.

The group-as-a-whole approach is sometimes criticized as being based on a faulty assumption. A group cannot be made responsible for conflicts because, "after decades of research and hundreds of investigations, there is nothing approaching consensus about what a therapeutic group is" (Kaul and Bednar 1986, p.710). Thus, if a group is not viewed as a specific entity that can feel, think, and behave, it certainly cannot cause conflict. Any group-as-a-whole intervention, such as a group process interpretation, runs the risk of being frankly delusional in its attempt to evoke a response from a recipient that in the final analysis is only an imaginary metapsychological construct.

Despite this criticism, however, a great mass of research is available on small-group processes (e.g. Hare 1976) supporting the group-as-a-whole approach as a viable alternative to other approaches of conflict transformation. One group-as-a-whole approach, based on the tradition of the Tavistock Institute of Human Relations in London (Miller and Rice 1967; Rice 1965), has been employed successfully around the world to manage conflicts in large groups (de Maré *et al.* 1991). Sociodrama as described in the present book is another example of this approach. Clearly, any practitioner who neglects the formidable group processes which operate in the development, maintenance, and resolution of intragroup conflicts disregards the very essence of group work.

Conclusion

Any conflict transformation effort must firmly acknowledge the intricate interplay between different levels of interpersonal conflict, suggesting that human aggression is caused by a complex web of related factors, including instinct, drive, physiological state, genetic makeup, individual developmental history, environmental provocation, and social situation (Bandura 1973). This interplay demands the employment of an integrative transformation strategy, which will be more effective than the use of any individual approach in isolation.

An integrative approach to conflict transformation (Heitler 1987; Tajfel and Turner 1986) must take into consideration more than one level, and frequently all levels, of understanding and intervention at various stages in the conflict-transformation process. Whether working within a psychodynamic or an action-oriented therapeutic framework, the conflict-transformation process spanning a few or many sessions should include some combination of ventilation, identification of individual issues, interpersonal reconciliation, and analysis of the group as a whole in combination. The omission of one level of intervention may leave the antagonists with unresolved tensions and the conflict transformation incomplete.

The levels of intervention seem to be arranged in a priority hierarchy, following a certain order of preference. As those on one level are resolved, those on the next take precedence. Thus, when the emotional needs of aggressive expression are satisfied, the needs of the intrapsychic exploration of personal preferences press for resolution. If some progress is made on this level, the interpersonal work on reciprocal interaction and communication will have more chance to succeed. Finally, if people are at peace with both their bodies and their minds and with each other, they can start to deal with more global group dynamic and social factors that bother them.

It is not easy to reconcile in one model several diverse approaches and to integrate them within one and the same group. The fundamental theoretical assumptions and treatment goals often seem to be contradictory. This contradiction, however, disappears as soon as the total picture is analyzed from all the points of view; and it is my experience that the four levels of conflict transformation can be made compatible with one another through the flexible employment of an integrative approach to conflict transformation. In the final analysis, anything less than such a global and holistic perspective is a reduction and simplification of the complex, multidimensional bio-physiological–emotional–organic–social systems involved in any conflict.

Obviously, conflicts are never totally resolved. After the expression of aggression, the intrapsychic exploration, the interpersonal negotiations, and the large-group system transformations, some amount of resentment based on the earlier conflict will remain in each person. Such residues of suspicion must be taken very seriously because they may easily erupt under certain circumstances and reignite the old conflict with new fuel. To prevent this, there is an enormous need, after the storm is over, to heal some of the emotional wounds in the population of both sides. Such healing includes not only the psychological needs of mourning the losses and working through the guilt but also a serious search for ways to reach some kind of inner and outer reconciliation with the former enemies in terms of truth commissions, the bringing of war criminals to justice, and postwar peace promotion initiatives. Such activities will be further discussed in the next chapter.

8

Postwar healing and reconciliation

For everything there is a season,
And a time for every matter under heaven:
A time to be born, and a time to die;
A time to plant, and a time to pluck up what is planted;
A time to kill, and a time to heal;
A time to break down, and a time to build up;
A time to weep, and a time to laugh;
A time to mourn, and a time to dance;
A time to throw away stones, and a time to gather stones together;
A time to embrace, and a time to refrain from embracing;
A time to seek, and a time to lose;
A time to keep, and a time to throw away;
A time to tear, and a time to sew;
A time to keep silence, and a time to speak;
A time to love, and a time to hate;
A time for war, and a time for peace.

(Ecclesiastes 3:1–8)

The book of Ecclesiastes tells the story of a man who searched for happiness without success. As he finally was ready to give up his quest and admit failure, he suddenly discovered that the search itself was a source of excitement and that much was gained during the entire journey. He realized that the satisfaction of life came from living it as fully as possible during its various seasons of birth and death, laughter and tears, war and peace and that there was "a time for every matter under heaven" (Ecclesiastes 3:1).

The same holds true for sociodrama. As described in earlier chapters, it can be employed in times of conflict and war and it can also be employed in times of peace when there is a need for postwar healing and reconciliation. This will be the focus of the present chapter. Such work deals with the painful residues of intergroup conflicts as they appear between two countries that earlier fought against each other.

Let us take the Vietnam War as an example. What did survivors need immediately at its end in 1973? And what do they need now? The immediate need of the Vietnamese survivors to mourn their millions of casualties was self-evident, as was the need to rebuild their country. The more long-term need of clearing the minefields was also obvious and urgent still today. On the other side of the conflict, the immediate needs of the US soldiers who returned home after the war were different from the needs of the local population. As shown in the film *Coming Home*, much of the soldiers' emotional lives had to be rebuilt as they returned home because their horrible experiences had disfranchised them from the ordinary lives of family and community (Shay 1994). Deep emotional scars were left in all participants of the war; some are surely still present on both sides of the conflict, creating an enormous need for post-trauma healing. Some of these survivors could be assisted with psychodrama, as described by Burge (2000) in the book on using psychodrama with trauma survivors (Kellermann and Hudgins 2000). In addition to the need for healing such individual scars, however, there was also a profound need for some kind of collective reconciliation between the people of the two countries. This process of rapprochement has been gradual. For example, a little more than 20 years after the end of the war, Vietnam and the USA established diplomatic relations. However, it was only in 2005 that trade relations and direct flights between the two countries resumed.

Can sociodrama be utilized for such a postwar healing and reconciliation process? What needs to be done on individual, small-group, large-group, and community levels to promote essential peace-promoting development? What are the possibilities for postwar reconciliation in survivors and their descendants immediately after the war, a few years later, a few decades later, and more than a century later?

Because the scars of war are always deep and painful and because they heal slowly, if at all, this postwar process of healing and normalization must be given special attention. Recent anniversaries illustrate the profound short- and long-term needs that remain in the various affected populations. For example, what do the Croat, Serb, and Bosnian people of the former Republic of Yugoslavia feel towards one another today, 10 or 15 years after the war? How do the various populations who survived the genocide in Rwanda feel? Is there still resentment left in the man from Phnom Penh who lost his mother, older sister, brother, and their families, all of whom had been clubbed to death by the Khmer Rouge in the killing fields of Cambodia 30 years earlier? And what does it mean for Holocaust survivors, 60 years after the Second World War, to attend a commemoration ceremony at Auschwitz in which the German chancellor publicly asks for forgiveness for what his people did to the Jews? What do the families of the victims of the atom bombs in Hiroshima and Nagasaki feel towards the US today? And what resentments remain in the descendants of the Sioux Indians more than 100 years after the massacre at Wounded Knee? Probably, most survivors would say they have not forgotten and they have not forgiven (Smedes 1984).

For example, in a society such as Northern Ireland, which has been struggling for centuries to overcome the effects of prolonged social violence (Fay, Morrissey and Smyth 1999), the concept of forgiveness is as relevant as ever. In the 1990s, a series of ceasefires by paramilitary groups on both sides led to the Good Friday Agreement. Article 2 (1998) stated:

> We must never forget those who have died or been injured, and their families. But we can best honour them through a fresh start, in which we firmly dedicate ourselves to the achievement of reconciliation, tolerance and mutual trust, and to the protection and vindication of the human rights of all.

This agreement received the support of 71 percent of the Northern Irish electorate in a referendum and led to the creation of a local assembly and a power-sharing government, embracing all the major political parties. After the euphoria following the agreement, however, the difficulties to be faced in achieving real peace became apparent.

Long-standing conflicts between people don't just disappear as a result of peace agreements. They continue to infect intergroup relations for a very long time. If there have been serious war crimes committed, such as torture and genocide, the split may be impossible to bridge. Survivors of oppression will continue to feel deep resentments against their perpetrators, even if there have been several overt gestures of reconciliation. For example, while the normalization process between Israel and Germany may be a huge step towards bridging the gap from the Second World War, within individual survivors of the Holocaust there will never be any complete reconciliation with the German people. This difficult process of normalization may continue for several more generations. On the other hand, between countries that fought on a more equal basis, such as Germany and England, the reconciliation process has been much more successful. Most of these former enemies have even been able to join together within the European Union, but that has still taken half a century after the Second World War.

In addition, six decades after the United States dropped atomic bombs on the Japanese cities of Hiroshima and Nagasaki, little animosity remains between the two nations. The war claimed about 400,000 US troops around the world, more than three times that many Japanese troops, and at least 300,000 Japanese civilians. But, out of the ashes, Japan and the United States have forged a close political alliance that has led to real peace and extensive cooperation.

Thus, there seems to be no objective reason why people cannot learn to live together again, even after a devastating war. Multi-ethnic groups have lived together in peace since time immemorial. To reach this stage of coexistence after war, however, requires some kind of active reconciliation process that goes beyond simple peace agreements. However, this need has been largely neglected in the past. Leaders have seemed more interested in how to make war than how to make peace and have often neglected to promote friendly coexistence after long-standing violent conflicts. After the peace treaties have been signed, citizens have been more or less left to themselves to rebuild a viable coexistence with their former enemies.

Postwar adjustment

Obviously, most survivors want to return to normal as fast as possible after the fighting has ended. Soldiers come home to their families, civilians who have been dislocated return to their villages and towns or immigrate to other countries, and people in general want to put the past behind them quickly. Often, this adjustment process proceeds too fast for the most victimized populations who cannot digest the sudden change. For them, it is impossible to switch one reality off and immediately switch another reality on. People who have been living in a dangerous world of shooting and killing are expected to adjust to a peaceful world of coexistence just days after the war ends. For most survivor populations, however, this adjustment will take many weeks, months, and years; and for a few it will take an entire lifetime or more. These people struggle not only with their own personal scars, but also with long-standing resentments toward their former oppressors and perpetrators.

For example, during a group session with survivors of Rwanda more than ten years after the war, participants shared both their personal and interpersonal agonies. They still had vivid memories of the terrible brutality pursued by the perpetrators, who used long knives to slaughter men, women, and children. Some had visible scars on their heads as overt reminders of their terrible ordeals. But they had not received any compensation and their suffering had not yet been acknowledged publicly. They were forced to live in close proximity with their torturers because the state and the church had declared that everybody must contribute to the reconciliation efforts. This, they said, was the most difficult task in their postwar adjustment. Often, however, other even more urgent problems, such as hunger and poverty, took precedence over the deep-seated resentments, and then the coexistence issues between Hutu and Tutsi became a little more bearable.

Psychosocial healing and peace building must be important parts of any postwar reconciliation process. Such elements should be viewed as being as important as material reconstruction in the aftermath of collective man-made trauma. In the past, however, while the international community provided postwar societies with various kinds of economic and political emergency assistance, followed by peacekeeping forces, little was done to provide war-torn societies with reconciliation assistance for future peace building.

This situation is slowly changing, however. Today the importance of postconflict healing for the general public of war-torn societies is more widely accepted. The international community now recommends various kinds of peace-making and reconciliation services as a part of postwar rebuilding assistance (Assefa 2001). In addition, relatively new methods of truth and reconciliation commissions have been developed, which are practiced regularly all over the world. In fact, they are often integral parts of the regular emergency services provided by international aid organizations and by nongovernmental organizations. For example, after the war in the former Republic of Yugoslavia, representatives of all ethnic groups (including Serb, Muslim, and Croat survivors) were invited to attend various postwar forums, reconciliation median groups, and post-trauma healing activities (e.g. Agger and Jensen 1996; Audergon 2005; Klain 1992; Tauber 2004; Wessells and Monteiro 2000). Such groups have been organized in many other war-stricken areas all over the world today, aimed at breaking the vicious cycle of suspicion, resentment, and revenge between former enemies.

A foremost proponent of dramatic methods to heal the wounds of history and to bring about reconciliation between groups in conflict is Armand Volkas, the founder the Center for the Living Arts in the US. His innovative programs have used drama therapy and expressive arts therapies for social change, intercultural conflict resolution, reconciliation, and intercultural communication for many years. As part of his reconciliation programs, he has worked with Palestinians and Israelis (Abu-Nimer 1999); Korean-Americans and Japanese-Americans; and African-Americans and European-Americans. At the heart of his work is a profound respect for the power of the personal story not only to heal deep emotional wounds but also to build bridges between people and cultures within a collective experience of mutual understanding. In a keynote speech from 2002 Volkas gave the following succinct description of what his postwar work is all about:

> My work with historical trauma is about a search for meaning. It is about memory and remembering. It is about sharing personal story and being witnessed. It is about how trauma is passed from generation to generation. It is about working through and integrating the complex emotions that arise when we face history in a personal way. It is about exploring what happens when the personal and collective come together – when one person's story becomes the story of an entire people. It is about grief and mourning. It is about remembering and honoring the dead. It is about acknowledging and owning the potential perpetrator in all of us. It is about building bridges between cultures. It is about cultural and national identity and self-esteem, for we all have a need to feel positive about the "tribe" to which we belong.

This description is an accurate and encompassing summary also of the message of the present book and the goals of reconciliation sociodrama.

A systematic and comprehensive model of reconciliation is the peace-building, conflict transformation and postwar reconstruction, reconciliation, and resolution (PCTR) method, based upon the TRANSCEND system for conflict transformation by peaceful means (Galtung 1996). It teaches the structures and dynamics of war and violent conflict, skills, tools, and approaches useful for peace building, conflict transformation, and postwar reconstruction, reconciliation, and healing. It also covers the effective development and implementation of peace-building strategies and conflict transformation at the local, national, and international levels. The method is designed for practitioners, political leaders, policy makers, and organizations working in areas affected by violent and nonviolent conflict and war, as well as in countries and regions in postwar situations. In discussing how people cope with the visible and invisible after-effects of war and violence, Galtung (1998) identified three essential tasks (called the 3R): reconstruction (after violence), reconciliation (of the conflict parties), and resolution (of the root conflict). By working on all three tasks in parallel, the former vicious cycles of violence may be transformed into new virtuous cycles of coexistence.

Sociodrama may be an alternative or complementary method for such postwar healing and reconciliation activities. It facilitates both individual and interpersonal processes of postwar adjustment. As such, it can be a companion to other approaches or function as the single approach for instigating some reconciliation between populations who were engaged in war. While the ambitious long-term goal in such groups is to find some balance and harmony between the earlier enemies, a more humble (and realistic) goal may be to instill a sense of hope in the parties and a belief in the possibility of a better future if peace is only preserved. Such a feeling may be developed from the practice of a few simple coexistence experiences that emphasize the similarities of all human beings and the advantages of living in a pluralistic, tolerant society rather than in a segregated, intolerant one. In addition, there may be an active search for ways to rebuild the old sense of "mixed" community often destroyed as a result of the war.

To achieve these goals, the following basic stages of postwar psychological healing within a sociodramatic setting may be initiated and worked through. First, participants are encouraged and assisted in finding some outlet for their pent-up emotions within a very safe, homogeneous group environment. Second, they face their various internalized prejudices seriously and explore them in depth to determine if these really hold up to reality. Third, when the time is ripe, the participants are slowly and sensitively introduced to their former enemies and urged to discuss their complicated relations openly to find a suitable balance between the status quo and reconciliation/forgiveness. Parallel to these three stages of reconciliation, there must be public community activities concerning the legal, historical, educational, and sociopolitical consequences of the war. Such activities are a necessary precondition for any significant progress in the individual and interpersonal postwar healing process. Finally, some reconciliation and peace-making rituals conclude the process of postwar psychological healing in a more spiritual fashion.

These five stages are presented in Box 8.1. They naturally draw on some of the principles discussed in earlier chapters and have some basic similarities to the conflict management approaches described in chapter 7, but they are here described within the specific setting of postwar healing and reconciliation.

Box 8.1 Stages of postwar healing and reconciliation

---

1.   emotional expression

2.   intrapsychic (representational) reconciliation

3.   intergroup (reciprocal) reconciliation

4.   community reconciliation

5.   peace-making ritual.

Emotional expression

Survivors are universally overwhelmed by mixed emotions at the end of the war. When the initial euphoria from having survived has faded, they face a cruel and sudden wake-up call. Though the outside war might be over, the same is not true for the inner world of the individual survivors. For them, this is just the beginning of the long process of "surviving survival." The enormous losses from the war are realized only gradually and a long mourning process is initiated, which sometimes continues for the rest of their lives. Those who are also burdened by feelings of guilt for not being able to protect their families and friends or for having inflicted injuries on others without sufficient justification may be similarly tormented. In addition, many suffer from a deep sense of humiliation (Lindner 2002).

Finally, those who have experienced war continue to anticipate the next one and always fear a new catastrophe may happen again at any moment. Any such previously traumatized individuals are bewildered when hearing bad news about hurricanes, mudslides, earthquakes, or the outbreak of some major pandemic. With an almost apocalyptic frame of reference, they ask themselves if the end is near (again) and what they need to do to protect themselves and their families from such a doomsday scenario this time. Some of these previously traumatized people might turn to religious leaders for guidance and comfort in such situations.

The most dominant emotional residues among survivors, however, are their all-encompassing feelings of resentment towards their (former) enemies. Such hostility remains a long time and may be accompanied by a desire for revenge that can be difficult to restrain. According to some trauma therapists (e.g. Gina Ross), the need to work through such deep-seated feelings of hate is especially important to stop the endless perpetuation of war in continuous cycles of violence and revenge. In addition, harboring such hate demands a heavy price because it is such a self-destructive force to bear.

These various emotional responses to major trauma have been described in detail in chapter 4, and we have suggested that crisis sociodrama is a suitable intervention strategy for this first phase of postwar healing. Psychodramatic reenactments of the major traumatic situation with an opportunity for emotional catharsis of pent-up feelings may, therefore, be the treatment of choice and provide sufficient initial relief for further intrapsychic reconciliation work.

Intrapsychic (representational) reconciliation

In addition to the need for finding emotional relief, survivors need to confront a variety of intrapsychic conflicts connected to the war. What was done to whom, by whom, in which circumstances, and for what reason? Such conflicts around self and other representations may also call for individual psychodramatic, rather than sociodramatic, interventions and have been addressed in the earlier volume on psychodrama with trauma survivors (Kellermann and Hudgins 2000). This stage is an important one because it urges representatives of one group to work through some of their unfinished business with the other group without the other group being present. The purpose is to help reconcile the parties to themselves, which sometimes includes inner forgiveness.

Forgiveness is an unfolding process that may require individuals to transition from the initial experience of intense pain through possible modification of the status of their relationships (Scobie and Scobie 1998). Benefits associated with such forgiveness (see McCullough, Pargament and Thoresen 2000, for a recent review) include:

- promoting self-respect by enabling the injured parties to refuse to let their lives be dominated by harmful thoughts, memories, and negative feelings (Holmgren 1993)

- finding release from resentment (Enright *et al.* 1996; North 1987)

- decreasing feelings of anger, anxiety, depression (Davenport 1991; Fitzgibbons 1986, 1998), guilt (Halling 1994), and revenge (Cloke 1993).

Immediately after the end of fighting, many survivors are totally immersed in their war trauma and remain detached from the current realities of day-to-day life for some time. Because of their terrible experiences, many view themselves as unworthy and are full of self-reproach and self-contempt. Others view themselves simply as different from other "normal" people, as if they come from another world. Such negative self-images must be dealt with before any interpersonal reconciliation can be initiated. If not, they will be a source of further interpersonal confusion and conflict because such survivors tend to project the negative internalized images upon the external world and to split people into either "good" and "bad" or "us" and "them" categories. Earlier chapters have discussed such general splitting tendencies, but they are intensified in recent survivors of war, torture, oppression, and persecution. In most such cases, survivors have a profound need to talk extensively about "what they did to us" and try to come to terms with the personal consequences of such maltreatment.

At one time or another during such explorations, the protagonist or the group of survivors will participate in an imaginary confrontation with the inner representations of the former perpetrators. They will be encouraged to express old resentments they hold against these tormentors. Such painful encounters are not done initially with the actual perpetrator but with another person who plays that role. A voluntary stand-in or a trained "auxiliary ego" is chosen for the absent "evil" person. Within the sociodramatic enactment, the former torture survivors are encouraged to express their feelings towards that person. For example, the family of victims of the September 11 terrorist attack may thus get an opportunity to confront auxiliaries playing the roles of the terrorists and of Osama bin Laden. Such externalization of the inner "evil" object serves to demarcate the "evil" object, which in itself may bring relief. Other therapeutic aspects of this therapy process have been fully described in my earlier book on psychodrama (Kellermann 1992).

At a later stage, survivors may need to contemplate the road to "intrapsychic reconciliation" and to reach some kind of inner forgiveness (Staub and Pearlman 2001). This is desirable because it liberates or puts to better use all the energy being used to hold the old resentments and provides some inner peace. The survivors also rediscover more affectionate aspects of themselves that they have long repressed. If successful, such vicarious and representational forgiveness may help survivors let go of the past and start to forgive themselves.

This kind of sociodramatic reconciliation work resembles Hellinger's (2002) systemic constellation approach, which partly evolved from Moreno's psychodrama and sociodrama. Hellinger also utilized participants from the group to represent absentees, including perpetrators of genocide and war. These figures were positioned in relation to each other in a significant manner; but, unlike sociodrama, they did not enact a specific role as described by the protagonist or the director, nor did they speak. They were simply asked intuitively to pose or move in a way that felt right for them in such a situation. The leader sometimes intervened and instructed them to stand, sit, or lie down at certain places and let the protagonist either watch it all from outside or enter into the situation and move it forward. Many such constellation sessions focused on one or the other theme of forgiveness and reconciliation based on ancient or recent war experiences. In these sessions, children might also be asked to bow down and honor their parents in a symbolic act of forgiveness.

Hellinger's family constellations seem to be based on the confession ceremony in Catholic Christianity. Contrary to what it looks like, however, Hellinger (2002) denied that this procedure advocates a request by the perpetrator for absolution, from the victims. "Forgiveness carries particularly bad consequences if the victim absolves the guilty party of their guilt, as if this was the victim's right. If there is to be a true reconciliation, then the innocent party has not only the right to reparation, but also the duty to demand it" (p.22).

This kind of intrapsychic work within the context of reconciliation sociodrama is a necessary step preceding any actual intergroup reconciliation work. Without it, the reciprocal reconciliation will have no chance to succeed and may even lead to more resentments than before. In addition, it is usually preferable to do any such preparatory intrapsychic (representational) work within a homogeneous group that does not have to respond to the feelings of the other. If, however, such work has been properly completed, the actual confrontations between former enemies or between victims and perpetrators will be less painful for both.

Intergroup (reciprocal) reconciliation

Obviously, reconciliation meetings between people who have been at war are very painful. After long negotiations and the signing of peace treaties, there is usually a "cooling off" period when the former enemies need some distance from one another, if possible, to recuperate from the violence.

Providing physical distance, however, is not always possible. In many postwar countries, such as in the former Republic of Yugoslavia and in Rwanda (Athanase 2001), enemies immediately had to start living together again after the fighting stopped. For those who returned to their (mixed) villages and towns, there was no choice but coexistence. Immediate reconciliation processes were urgently needed to prevent the former enemies from initiating new cycles of violence. Survivors of oppression and torture met their perpetrators on a daily basis. The group from Rwanda complained that they were overwhelmed with frustration when seeing neighbors who had taken part in the genocide going about their business as if nothing had happened.

Within such explosive areas of postwar tension, complicated intergroup conflicts perpetually arise, including those concerning education, economy, politics, and culture. Therefore, platforms for community interchange within public forums to discuss these issues are needed immediately. These platforms may be initiated within diplomatic missions, interreligious committees, cultural interchange programs, etc. to keep the fragile dialogue going, clear up possible misunderstandings before they lead to new violence, and discuss possible residues of the old conflict in a formal atmosphere.

Such discussions are usually held only within the closed settings of politicians and functionaries. Sociodrama for reconciliation, however, is open for everybody; ordinary people get an opportunity to present their concerns and to search for their own solutions to interpersonal and community problems. Sometimes, these groups are more easily formed by women and only for women. Then they deal only with issues of concern to women. Because women have usually not participated in the actual fighting and present common concerns about child care, housekeeping, and family problems in an atmosphere of cooperation, these groups become the cornerstones of society and future bridges to a new coexistence (e.g. there was a time, even in the former Palestine, when Jewish and Arab women breast-fed their children together as extended family).

When former adversaries participate in a sociodrama session, Moreno's original concept of encounter forms a viable structure for the dialogues. This structure includes not only an honest meeting between two equal parties but also an alternative way of dealing with oneself and with other people based on honesty, awareness, choice, and body acceptance (Schutz 1973). It is guided by the vision of a humane, egalitarian, and just society based on the principles of acceptance, trust, and nonviolence. According to Hewstone (1996), there are four possible types of such intergroup encounters. The first is contact that emphasizes the uniqueness of every individual, such as in classical psychodrama. It uses the encounter to search for things that unite rather than divide the participants. The second is intergroup contact, which emphasizes the group rather than the individual and which improves the ability to generalize, such as in classical sociodrama. The third is crossed categorization contact, which emphasizes more than one component of the identities of the groups in the encounter. Finally, the fourth is recategorization contact, the goal being to create one common identity for everyone in a kind of melting pot. These different types of contact offer two general options for long-term reconciliation: the first is to divide the group into its individual components, stressing what the participants share in common as individuals; and the second option is to strengthen the group as a whole to improve the communication and the intergroup interaction between its participants.

The truth, however, is that former enemies rarely meet face to face after a war. Groups that have mutually harmed each other in the past are seldom brought together to share their feelings. If such meetings do occur, they are initiated many years after the original violence and for purposes that are not explicitly focused on reconciliation. For example, war veterans from both sides who fought against one another during the Second World War met for the first time at the 60-year commemoration ceremonies in 2005. There have also been a few exceptional attempts in which former perpetrators and victims have come together after many years to try to understand what happened in the past, but the actual participants of war usually never meet face to face.

As a result, such meetings have been left for their children. For example, while their parents who participated in that war could not meet face to face, children of Holocaust survivors and of Nazi perpetrators have met occasionally during the last few decades in long-term dialogue groups in Europe, the US, and Israel to talk about their common past. In addition, blacks and whites in the US (Helmes 1990), South Africa, and elsewhere have discussed their common history. Similarly, Israelis and Palestinians in the Middle East (Abu-Nimer 1999; Halaby, Sonnenschein and Friedman 2000), various ethnic subgroups of the former Yugoslavia, and mixed groups of Hutu and Tutsi in Rwanda/Burundi have also attempted such shorter or longer reconciliation and conflict resolution groups, often organized and funded by international foundations. Finally, an inspiring collection of stories of how ordinary men and women, active in women's groups, youth groups, and faith-based organizations, have played a crucial part in conflict prevention and peace building was published by van Tongeren et al. (2005).

Reconciliation methods must naturally be adjusted to local conditions. In Rwanda, for example, leaders found the pure verbal methods inadequate and a variety of expressive art techniques was tried, with later reflections and discussions of the material presented. Kester (2001) provided some evidence of the relative success of these programs. An interesting outcome was that those who had participated in the groups were more willing to forgive perpetrators on the condition that they acknowledge what they had done.

Such face-to-face encounters between former enemies, with the purpose of some kind of forgiveness, are important for any real reconciliation process. The closest things to such groups are the various truth and reconciliation commissions (TRC), which are a relatively new phenomenon, starting only in the 1980s. A list of 24 such commissions may be found at http://www.usip.org/library/truth.html. One of the first and most well-known commissions was held in South Africa. On his appointment as chairperson of the Truth and Reconciliation Commission on November 30 1995, Archbishop Tutu said:

> I hope that the work of the Commission, by opening wounds to cleanse them, will thereby stop them from festering. We cannot be facile and say bygones will be bygones, because they will not be bygones and will return to haunt us. True reconciliation is never cheap, for it is based on forgiveness, which is costly. Forgiveness in turn depends on repentance, which has to be based on an acknowledgement of what was done wrong, and therefore on disclosure of the truth. You cannot forgive what you do not know… (Tutu 2000)

The TRC aims to facilitate a truth recovery process through public hearings that give voice to the experiences of victims, witnesses, and perpetrators, attempting to uncover the causes, nature, and extent of past human rights violations and to search for ways to rehabilitate and to compensate the victims for their suffering. In addition, the TRC gives amnesty to certain perpetrators of abuse who can prove that their crimes were politically motivated and that they disclosed the relevant information concerning their actions. In the case of South Africa, the TRC gave a voice to those who had earlier not spoken, the victims of the past, and the survivors of the present; and nobody could escape listening. At one point, Desmond Tutu broke down and sobbed before his nation. After that, many South Africans started to look at their neighbors in a new way.

Truth commissions provide a sense of validation and a feeling of not being alone, but they do not provide the necessary therapeutic process for the collective healing of emotional trauma. While it might be comforting to give testimony and to participate in communal ceremonies, this in itself does not make it easier to come to terms with the past. I believe that a suitable combination of psychodramatic and sociodramatic group sessions can be a very powerful complementary tool for such truth commissions. These sessions are important not only as an additional trauma therapy instrument for the survivors themselves but also as an additional reconciliation tool for the group members who become active participants in the drama about the past and in the present lives of the protagonists on a very deep level. As a result, the other person is often regarded as a "human being" for the first time since the end of the war.

In a series of publications, Volkan (1988, 1997, 1999) described his intergroup dialogue work with representatives of Arab and Israeli, Russian and Estonian, Turk and Greek, Turk and Armenian, Serb and Croatian, and Georgian and South Ossetian groups. He observed that when representatives of enemies came together for a series of dialogues for unofficial negotiations, usually meeting every three months over some years, they evolved as spokespersons of their large group's shared sentiments. During such meetings, he noted that sentiments close to concepts of apology and forgiveness were related to what he named an "accordion phenomenon." This phenomenon refers to a repeated accordion pattern of squeezing together and then pulling apart in which opposing participants suddenly experience a rapprochement that is followed by a sudden withdrawal from one another. He assumed that derivatives of aggression within the opposing groups underlie this phenomenon. Because each party brings its mental representations of historical injuries, the initial distancing is thus a defensive maneuver to keep aggressive attitudes and feelings in check. If the opponents come too close, they may harm one another or become targets of retaliation.

We therefore have to accept that the process of reconciliation is a long and difficult one requiring continuous efforts with only small steps of progress at a time (Dajani and Carel 2002). There are no shortcuts to this difficult process; it cannot be forced or rushed without serious consideration of the real disrepancies that exist between the groups in conflict. It is essential that any reconciliation process must progress at a slow pace, one step at a time, without any pressure for premature resolutions. According to Volkan (2002):

> Those individuals who call themselves practitioners of international "conflict resolution" may in fact do harm if they force the removal of identity differences between large groups as swiftly as possible or focus on seeking "apologies" and encouraging "forgiveness" too hastily when dealing with coexistence and related issues.

Reconciliation groups often function within a philosophy of cross-cultural understanding and peace building. For example, the School for Peace in the Jewish–Arab village of Neve Shalom/Wahat al-Salam has conducted inter-group dialogue groups on a regular basis since 1979. They believe that, while such groups cannot change the political reality, they can change the partici-pants' awareness of this reality and thus help to improve the understanding of Jewish–Palestinian relations. The hope is that such understanding will motivate participants to promote social and political change in their immediate surroundings and thus prepare the ground for large-scale change over the long term. Halaby and Sonnenschein (2004) wrote:

> The School for Peace has always challenged the inter-personal approach of coexistence projects, claiming that they serve to sweep problems under the rug and to preserve the existing inequalities and discrimina-tory power relations between Jews and Arabs. Here we must stress that even encounters that are done "the right way", on the intergroup basis, cannot change our reality. Economic and political forces created this reality, and only these forces can change it. (p.374)

As a result of such observations, there can be no complete postwar healing or reconciliation without a real effort to settle the differences in a just and fair manner within the public setting of community reconciliation. The various legal, historical, educational, and sociopolitical consequences of peace-making must therefore be settled within the larger setting of the community at a macrosociological level.

Community reconciliation

Postwar community reconciliation is a complicated public process that includes a fair peace settlement, justice, accountability, responsibility, and public commemoration. While ordinary people can make a difference in a bottom-up approach to intragroup reconciliation, primarily governments within a top-down approach have a responsibility to implement these public tasks. The following tasks are all necessary but are not sufficient conditions for reconciliation.

The first task is to reach a fair peace settlement. Recent armed conflicts in the Persian Gulf, Bosnia, Rwanda, and Kosovo demonstrate the difficulty and illustrate the importance of ending wars in a fair fashion. We know that when wars are wrapped up badly they sow the seeds for future bloodshed. Governments have, therefore, decided upon certain basic rules that have to be followed in how to end a war and to ease the transition from war back to peace. The most obvious is, of course, a just peace settlement, which secures the basic rights to life and liberty of all the people involved in the conflict. (Examples of such settlements with a regularly updated "Peace Agreements Digital Collection" can be found online at http://www.usip.org/library/pa.html.)

Because there is no such peace in Darfur at the time of writing, what the population needs there more than anything else is a strong peace agreement between the citizens and their government. This agreement should make sure that the government never again gets the power to exterminate its own people. But peace talks have gone nowhere, largely because the international community has paid too little attention to them.

The second task is to obtain justice. This task is based on the question asked by the late Nazi hunter Simon Wiesenthal: "How can the survivors sleep well during the night when the criminals are still at large?" The question implies that without justice there can be neither reconciliation nor postwar trauma healing. The International Criminal Court at The Hague is one way of holding those who commit atrocities responsible for their crimes. Democratic states must reiterate the principles of accountability to reestablish themselves as moral authorities that can claim to represent oppressed communities (Borneman 1997).

While leaders of the regime who have been blatant violators of basic rights face public trials for war crimes and soldiers from all sides of the conflict who committed war crimes are also held accountable, innocent civilians should be kept out of such punitive postwar processes. Proportional financial restitution to victims, however, should be the responsibility of the entire society of the perpetrator nation. Finally, some kind of postwar rehabilitation and reform of the defeated country is often needed. This not only involves disarmament but also includes human rights education and some kind of democracy training.

For various reasons, however, many perpetrators of war crimes never get accused. If the perpetrators have not been put to justice, the victims feel let down by society for a second time – the first when the actual crime occurred and the second when it was not punished. Sometimes, there is also a lack of acknowledgement that the crime occurred in the first place. It is felt by the survivors that the world seems to look the other way when people are killed. It happened during the Holocaust during the Second World War and in Rwanda in 1994, as well as during the Armenian genocide of 1915, the Cambodian genocide of the 1970s, and the Bosnian massacres of the 1990s. In each case, statesmen said that, at the time it happened, they did not fully comprehend the scope of the genocides and that they were unable then to do anything to prevent them. Now the same tragedy is unfolding in Darfur.

The third task is to organize some suitable public commemoration for the victims. Such commemorations may include state ceremonies at anniversary dates, public memorials at central town locations, war museums, and public announcements of historical facts. These commemoration acts are in themselves a helpful facet of postwar healing for survivors and a counterforce to the tendency of communities to look only to the future and to forget about the past. Especially when crimes have been committed against humanity and there is an effort on the part of governments to conceal them, the need for public announcements of what happened is greatly increased.

For example, in the former communist USSR, where information was systematically concealed for more than half a century, there is currently an effort to open the archives and document the various crimes committed during the communist regime. Within the organization Memorial, there is a museum, a repository of documents, and a number of specialized libraries that attempt to preserve the societal memory of the political persecutions in the former Soviet Union.

The Russians, however, were not the only ones to conceal unpleasant information. Americans were for many years similarly unwilling to reveal to the general public the terrible effects of the atom bomb in Nagasaki. Though George Weller, a correspondent for the *Chicago Daily News*, photographed the terrible devastation, these photos remained unpublished for many years. And the Japanese were also guilty of trying to whitewash wartime atrocities against their neighbors during the Second World War. As a result, more than 10,000 Chinese students protested in Beijing in 2005, claiming that Japan had failed to appropriately deal with its wartime historic aggression.

A contrary approach was chosen in the Truth and Reconciliation Missions of South Africa. Mandela was one of the few political leaders who understood that the truth must be heard for the population to heal their collective wounds. Any public acts of commemoration facilitate such postwar healing and reconciliation processes. When survivors of war feel that the world remembers, they let time take its course and they can start to forget. In a paradoxical fashion, when people are urged by society to remember in a concerted community effort, they will also start to forget.

Public apologies by statesmen naturally have a special healing effect in such situations and may be very important in promoting local and international reconciliation.

While these components of community reconciliation are necessary preconditions for reconciliation, they are usually insufficient for a complete postwar trauma resolution. Because when a fair peace settlement has been reached, when war criminals have been brought to justice, and when the society has appropriately commemorated the victims, the survivors are still left with their own pain. None of these public gestures has brought their families back to life. As a result, there is still a need for some kind of symbolic peace-making rituals, which can move the postwar trauma resolution work towards its completion.

Peace-making rituals

Such rituals are an integral part of sociodrama and have profound and remarkable effects on its participants. Within a sociodrama for community reconciliation, groups may stage simulated peace treaties and mock trials of perpetrators; and they may organize symbolic concretizations of memorials. While survivors probably prefer that such reconciliation rites are actualized in reality and performed in public, these sessions still make a great deal of difference to the individual participants, who feel that their situations are finally acknowledged. These symbolic acts also have a multiplying effect, spreading the word, which may include deliberate efforts to affect public opinion and the attitudes of policy makers.

Sociodrama lends itself excellently for using peace-promoting rituals as an important final step in the postwar reconciliation process. As already explained in my previous book on psychodrama, the potential of various healing rituals based on role-playing and "as if" is enormous (Kellermann 1992). "Imagination allows for hope and dreams to re-enter our lives, even if only for a moment" (p.109). As realized by all religions and by various cultures, this same power can be harnessed for reconciliation after war. Such rituals may be based on Christian, Quaker, Buddhist, Muslim, Native American, African, or Gandhian principles for example and provide unique opportunities for gaining spiritual reconciliation.

Ritual helps people heal after a collective trauma and transcend to another level of intergroup balance. Ritual guides behavior and offers meaning and closure to the past. Ritual strengthens the link of the individual to the social group and to the culture at large (Durkheim 1961; Turner 1967). Ritual plays an important role, especially for traumatized individuals who have lost their sense of meaning in the world and who have isolated themselves from other people. The ceremony binds people together again, giving them new hope that their insurmountable problems can be overcome.

A variety of peace-making rituals have, therefore, been used both in the East and in the West to promote reconciliation and postwar healing. The Native American ritual of smoking the peace pipe is perhaps the most familiar ceremony. By sharing the peace pipe, a common bond of spiritual unity is established. The Hawaiian *Ho-O-Pono-Pono* (setting straight) ritual is another healing and conflict resolution procedure based on local community conflict resolution practices. In Uganda, the Acholi people use raw eggs, twigs, and livestock in their traditional reconciliation ceremonies when members of one tribe have killed members of another tribe. The *barisaa*, prayer tree, is an important site of worship in Siberian/Mongolian shamanism. It calls the nature spirits to bring inspiration, calm people's hearts, and create thoughts of peace and love. In Rwanda, traditional community courts with village elders, called *gacaca*, are used to solve disputes. Finally, Native American veterans are assisted in returning to their society through participation in a Navajo ritual called the Enemy Way. It lasts for seven days and involves family, clan, and community members in a ceremony that restores harmony, balance, and connection to the traumatized Navajo veteran (Parson 1985; 1990).

Depending on the culture of the conflicting parties, reconciliation sociodrama can utilize any of these ritual practices because they have inherent meanings to the participants. In most such sessions, the word *sociodrama* is not mentioned.

Reconciliation sociodrama is an alternative intervention strategy to facilitate the overall process of peace building and normalization after war. Such groups may be initiated during various stages of the postwar adjustment process. However, many aspects of reconciliation sociodrama are still unclear, including variables that may be assumed to influence such groups. Because there has not been any significant documentation of such groups and little can be learned from cumulative experience, there is still much to do to develop these practices. The only thing that we can be sure of is that no reconciliation process will be simple. The crueler the war and the more pain inflicted, the deeper the scars and the longer the healing process.

9

Retrospect and prospect

Sociodrama has had its ups and downs. There have been periods when it was more in vogue and other times when it disappeared into oblivion. I believe that we are now again in a time of growing interest; the practice of sociodrama is becoming more relevant than ever and it is also more widely used in countries all over the world. The future seems to hold great promise. After half a century of sociodrama, only now are we coming into our stride. At last, we are taking ourselves seriously, trying to document our work and setting standards for training and practice.

Why has it taken so long? Where are we going now that we have come this far? What is the future of sociodrama and what can we expect it to contribute to the world as it is developing for the next millennium? It is only with one eye focused on the future and the other looking back to the past that we can anticipate what new direction sociodrama may take.

In these days of frequent disasters, genocides, and wars, and with a greater awareness of their tragic psychological consequences, the need for sociodrama is increasing. The general opinion of the importance of war tribunals and truth commissions for the healing of the community has also contributed to the increased interest in sociodrama.

Admittedly, however, sociodrama might be a little too dramatic for many people who are more comfortable with the restrained procedures of the church or more familiar with the sanguine behaviors of the courthouse. In addition, sociodrama may be seen as too ambitious because it tries to deal with a tremendous number of problematic events with an approach that is primarily psychosocial and which can only briefly explore the various political and historical realities. With these reservations in mind, however, sociodrama is ordinarily responding to urgent community needs and it is based on a profound desire to help people make some sense of the misery and tragedy of the human condition. Because, in a world that has become much smaller due to globalization, people have become increasingly interested in investigating how things are connected and how various political decisions affects "us and them" in the present and the future. In the present global community, where individuals constantly move from one country to another, sociodrama can make a significant contribution to help integrate newcomers, and help refugees and immigrants to adjust to their new home environments. Furthermore, because of the vast cultural changes in our societies, new social problems have been created that call for active and powerful approaches such as sociodrama. We are required to make cities more harmonious, reduce crime rates, improve welfare, overcome racism, and increase the sense of responsibility of ordinary citizens, just to mention a few social challenges in the present world.

Clearly, however, we have a long way to go in bridging the gap between what is desired and what is possible and what is needed and what is available. Too few practitioners of sociodrama are available to provide for the enormous needs of the global community. While there are several sociodramatists who work in the fields of human relations and intergroup conflicts, very few of them meddle in actual sociopolitical matters. It is therefore important to initiate intense and high-quality sociodrama training for additional practitioners and to provide more specialized practice and appropriate supervision in any or all of the various applications described throughout this book.

With such specialized training, there are a number of settings in which sociodramatists could make a significant contribution and there are many applications that still have not been sufficiently developed; from organizational consulting to spiritual and religious reconciliation to innovative educational projects to the creative expression of the collective unconscious. For example, in a recent paper on sociodrama as a powerful tool in higher education, Blatner (2006) emphasized the surplus value of this active approach in making any learning more effective. As compared with a straightforward lecture from a professor, even a short sociodramatic role-playing exercise would make the subsequent discussion so much richer and deeper and the entire learning experience would become much more inspiring.

Some of these new avenues of practice, however, will inevitably force us to redefine our functions (as group therapists, clinicians, dramatists, and/or educators) and to be more flexible with our goals. As the world is changing, sociodrama will also change and mature. While nobody can know for sure where all this will lead us, we constantly have to adapt to new situations that are always more complex and surprising. Perhaps sociodrama will go not to one place but to many. That would be a welcome development. As most such methods, sociodrama will move with the ebb and flow of the interest of the crowds. Thus it was for Shakespeare in Elizabethan times; thus it was for Moreno during his lifetime; and thus it will be again in the future. In the meantime, we have no choice but to continue to be creative inventors and set our own goals as we go along.

Another reason for the slow development of sociodrama is that it is such a difficult undertaking. Not only is sharing collective pain with others is not only an emotionally overwhelming experience, but being witness to the tragedy of humankind may also cause vicarious traumatization. At the very least, it will evoke some sense of identification and grief in many people. One participant said:

> I got to know these people in a very special way. First I heard where they were coming from. I was amazed by the many different cultural origins of the members of this group. They came from India, Russia, Egypt, Turkey, Italy, Germany, Ireland, America, South America, Australia, and from many other places. Through them, I heard about the histories of their peoples, and especially about all their different misfortunes during the last century. There seemed to have been so many earthquakes, wars, massacres and famines all over the world. As we listened to all the sad stories, we all wept. So many people had been killed. Then those who hadn't been killed were homeless and they were starving. Then we heard about the natural disasters, and so it went on without interruption until we could not take in any more. There was so much suffering and disease and torture and horror and madness and despair... We all sobbed through it all.

All this is so much more difficult, since we read the papers and watch the news, and hear that these things are still happening all around the world. People continue to kill and be killed; 20 persons today, 200 tomorrow, 2000 next week, 200,000 next month, 2,000,000 next year, and so on. Perhaps we also will be wiped out next time?

With a certain sense of hopelessness, we realize that tragedy is our common predicament. It is what is universal in us as human beings. It colors our spirit and it goes beyond our own lives and the lives of our own people. It cannot be destroyed and it will live on long after we have left this earth. It occurs, quietly and naturally all the time. Acknowledging it and expressing its accompanying emotions will always be a part of the sharing in any sociodrama group. In such groups we do not deal with trivial matters and usually there are no happy endings. These groups resemble a kind of a religious service, within which people pray together in silence for a better world with others. In comparison with such communal and spiritual gatherings, however, we sometimes want to turn to the Almighty not to worship but to express our outrage. We want to blame Him for the nightmare of the history of humankind. But if we do there will be nobody out there to respond. Instead, we will be met only with silence. Like a psychoanalyst behind the couch, God will not respond directly to our lamentations and we will be left only with an echo of our own utterances. As a result, there is no choice but to take responsibility for our own concerns.

Thus, when bad things happen that make us feel overwhelmed, powerless, and anxious, we cannot simply pray and hope for the best and place our trust in God's hands. It is precisely in such difficult times that we need to become more self-reliant and active and realize that we can do something by ourselves to influence our lives. Even after having experienced a devastating event, we yearn to be able to determine our own fate because our future and the future of human civilization depend on it. When everything seems to have been lost and we contemplate surrender, we need to look towards a brighter future (whether ten minutes or 100 years hence) as an open book to be written as a consequence of our own choices and not merely as inevitable "acts of God". We must start to realize that we are collectively responsible for what we do with this earth and with our lives. With such an attitude of co-creators of the universe, we will be at least as responsible for the destiny of humankind as God Himself.

As a global community, we need to become more "able-to-respond" adequately to new catastrophic situations and to respond in new ways to old disasters. In short, we need to become more spontaneous. This is the essence of J. L. Moreno's philosophy and the ultimate purpose of sociodrama.

Survival

Darwin emphasized that people must adapt to the environment to survive. It is often forgotten, however, that, because all human life is social in nature, people survive not only because of their ability to adjust to outer difficulties, but also because of their ability to coexist with others as a group. It is the principle of the survival of the affiliate in addition to the survival of the fittest, a principle that Moreno (1953) emphasized in his book *Who Shall Survive?*

To illustrate this idea, Grete Leutz (1991), a student of Moreno from Germany and a leading international psychodramatist, told the following story about Moreno. As they were traveling back to Beacon from New York after an evening session, Moreno said to Leutz: "Look at all these people who are walking on the street. They all seem to be individual persons. But everybody is also a part of a social network. They have relations to significant other people who care about them. These relations make them sad or happy, worried or relaxed, angry or enthusiastic. Some of these people give them reason to live, others to die. Despite this fact – that their relations are a question of life and death – the scientific community doesn't consider this variable an important one for investigation. Even though it is often the most important one of all."

The principal is simple, but its implementation almost impossible. The interpersonal relations which are vital for our survival are the same as the ones that create so much trouble. As described in chapter 2, the greatest dangers for human beings are other human beings; and survival is nothing obvious.

Moreno's response to the question "Who shall survive?" was that "everyone should survive" (1953, p.607). But how?

In simple words, Moreno suggested that the survival of humankind depended upon a few simple principles of human coexistence. During his lifetime, he developed these into a whole theory and technique of interpersonal groupings and preferences – sociometry. Sociometry was based on the fact that people were social beings who liked to live together with others in herds or groupings (such as families; small groups; larger religious, geographical, and/or ethnic communities; and societies) rather than in isolation. Depending on how such entities were set up, they either improved or interfered with the lives of their individual members. Because human beings tend to be attracted to people of their own kind and reject those who are different, Moreno felt that harmonious social arrangements should be based on the freedom of people to choose the group to which they want to belong.

All people probably want to live in such a sociometrically balanced society. In this ideal system of coexistence, people would support one another with positive interpersonal relations, or "social atom energy," as Moreno liked to call it. The great power inherent in such relations would be a kind of counterforce to the threat of isolation and alienation, as well as conflict and intergroup tension. Within each large society, there would be thousands and thousands of such close relations, or social networks, that would counteract such a threat and, within each small (indivisible) network or "social atom," there would be people who cared for one another sufficiently to provide the support so vital for survival in times of stress and disaster. In effect, such strong bonds would leave their mark forever and help us withstand any trauma or "evil" force.

Unfortunately, however, there is still insufficient social atom energy available to withstand the various threats to humankind. The need, therefore, for active community approaches, such as sociodrama, to build powerful inter-personal support networks is still vast.

It is my hope that this book will help us take another step forward towards the human relations revolution that Moreno envisioned. In so doing, we might perhaps be able to ease some of the plentiful emotional pain that is created when different groups of the human species clash.

Final comments

In an interview with Marcia Karp (2000), Zerka Moreno told the following story about Moreno:

> ...at one point, about four years before he died, he [Moreno] was somewhat disillusioned in his ability to reach the larger world. He really had hoped to create a sociometric revolution; a revolution in human relations. However, when death was approaching he became more realistic. I sat by his bedside – trying not to cry because he was telling me that he was satisfied with what he had achieved. As to Moreno's philosophy, I think the answer is yes; it has all sorts of possibilities. I think it has not begun to be mined yet – his legacy – and people don't appreciate sufficiently the tremendous flexibility of this approach in many different fields. He was years ahead – maybe a century ahead – of his time. (p.28)

After having read some of the chapters of the present book, Zerka Moreno sent the following comments in July 2006:

> Considering my medical history when I fell and broke my hip in Riga on 9/11/2000 [sic], which eventuated into 5 surgeries and other complications, I am doing well at age 89…
>
> As I read some of the chapters of your book, the Jerusalem session in 2000 returned afresh to my mind. Unhappily, the current events in northern Israel and Lebanon underscore the worst parts of the problem once again in horrific fashion. In spite of the brave way the conflict was being presented by Teresa and Marcia, and the implications we carried with us, as well as the hope that we would like to see such events dealt with in sociodrama, it has not taken place on a larger scale.

Nevertheless I appreciate your view and thank you for having written your book. In these times it is very hard to hold on to hope. But what other choice is there?

A compendium of my writings has just been published by Routledge (Moreno 2006). Ironically, my very first paper, in 1944, dealt with the conflict between the role of the civilian and that of the soldier, in personal terms. Oh how I wish it were no longer relevant! What would this world of ours be like if Moreno had been given a chance to prove his point on a larger scale? Is it too much to assume that some of the wars and miseries we are now still witnessing might have been avoided? In any event, we must continue to carry his ideas to as many people as we can.

Sociodrama has an important role to play in bringing creativity and spontaneity back to all the citizens of our much threatened globe.

Love to you all

Zerka

References

Abu-Nimer, M. (1999) *Dialogue, conflict resolution, and change: Arab–Jewish encounters in Israel*. Albany, NY: State University of New York Press.

Adams, D. (1989) "The Seville statement on violence and why it is important." *Journal of Humanistic Psychology 29*, 328–337.

Agazarian, Y. and Carter, F. (1993) "Discussions on the large group." *Group 17*, 210–234.

Agazarian, Y. and Peters, R. (1981) *The visible and invisible group*. London: Routledge and Kegan Paul.

Agger, I. and Jensen, S.B. (1996) *Trauma and healing under state terrorism*. London: Zed Books.

Aguiar, M. (1998) *Teatro espontaneo e Psicodrama [Psychodrama and spontaneous theatre]*. Sao Paulo: Agora.

American Psychiatric Association (1994) *Diagnostic and statistical manual of mental disorders: DSM-IV*, 4th edn. Washington, DC: American Psychiatric Association.

Amir, Y. (1976) "The role of intergroup contact in change of prejudice and ethnic relations." In P.A. Katz (ed.) *Toward the elimination of racism*. New York: Pergamon.

Argyle, M. (1991) *Cooperation: the basis of sociability*. London: Routledge.

Ascher, I. and Shokol, A. (1976) "Maxwell Jones as facilitator in a therapeutic community." *Group Process 6*, 149–162.

Assefa, H. (2001) "Reconciliation." In L. Reychler and T. Paffenholz (eds) *Peace building: a field guide*. Boulder, CO: Lynne Rienner Publishers.

Athanase, H. (2001) "After genocide in Rwanda: social and psychological consequences." New York: Institute for the Study of Genocide. Available at: http://www.isg-iags.org/oldsite/newsletters/25/athanse.html.

Audergon, A. (2005) *The war hotel: psychological dynamics in violent conflict*. London: Whurr.

Axelrod, R. (1984) *The evolution of cooperation*. New York: Basic Books.

Ayoub, C. (2002) "In the aftermath of collective tragedy: why ending trauma's cycle starts here." *Harvard Graduate School of Education News*, 1 June. Cambridge, MA: Harvard University. Available at: http://www.gse.harvard.edu/news/features/ayoub06012002.html.

Bach, G. (1974) "Fight with me in group therapy." In L.R. Wolberg and M.L. Aronson (eds) *Group therapy 1974: an overview*. New York: Stratton.

Bach, G. and Goldberg, H. (1974) *Creative aggression*. New York: Avon.

Bales, R.F. (1970) *Personality and interpersonal behavior*. New York: Holt, Rinehart and Winston.

Bateson, G. (1979) *Mind and nature: a necessary unity*. New York: Dutton.

Bandura, A. (1973) *Aggression: a social learning analysis*. Englewood Cliffs, NJ: Prentice-Hall.

Bandura, A. and Walters, R.H. (1965) *Social learning and personality development*. New York: Holt, Rinehart and Winston.

Bauer, Y. (2001) *Rethinking the Holocaust*. New Haven, CT: Yale University Press.

Baytos, L.M. (1995) *Designing and implementing successful diversity programs.* Englewood Cliffs, NJ: Prentice-Hall.

Beck, A. (1999) *Prisoners of hate: the cognitive basis of anger, hostility, and violence.* New York: HarperCollins.

Berkowitz, L. (1989) "Frustration–aggression hypothesis: examination and reformulation." *Psychological Bulletin 106,* 59–73.

Bion, W.R. (1961) *Experience in groups and other papers.* London: Tavistock.

Bisno, H. (1988) *Managing conflict.* London: Sage.

Blatner, A. (2006) "Enacting the new academy: sociodrama as a powerful tool in higher education." *ReVision: A Journal of Consciousness and Transformation 29,* 3, 30–35.

Blood, R.O. (1960) "Resolving family conflicts." *Journal of Conflict Resolution 4,* 209–219.

Bloomfield, L. and Leiss, A.C. (1969) *Controlling small wars: a strategy for the 1970s.* New York: Knopf.

Bloomfield, L. and Moulton, A. (1997) *Managing international conflict: from theory to policy.* New York: St. Martin's Press/Worth Publishers.

Boal, A. (1979) *Theatre of the oppressed.* New York: Urizen.

Boal, A. (1992) *Games for actors and non-actors.* London: Routledge.

Borneman, J. (1997) *Settling accounts: violence, justice, and accountability in post-socialist Europe.* Princeton, NJ: Princeton University Press.

Boszormenyi-Nagy, I. and Spark, G.M. (1973) *Invisible loyalties: reciprocity in intergenerational family therapy.* Hagerstown, MD: Harper and Row.

Boutros-Ghali, B. (1992) *An agenda for peace: preventive diplomacy, peacemaking and peacekeeping.* New York: United Nations.

Bradshaw-Tauvon, K. (2001) "Spanning social chasms: inner and outer sociodramas." *The British Journal of Psychodrama and Sociodrama 16,* 23–28.

Brain, P.F. (1979) "Hormones and aggression." Annual Research Reviews. *Hormones and Aggression 2.* Montreal: Eden Press.

Brecht, B. (1963) *Schriften zum Theater.* Frankfurt: Suhrkamp.

Buer, F. (1991) "Editorial." *Jahrbuch für psychodrama, psychosoziale praxis and gesellschaftspolitik.* Opladen: Leske and Budrich.

Burge, M. (2000) "Psychodrama with Vietnam veterans and their families: both victims of traumatic stress." In P.F. Kellermann and K. Hudgins (eds) *Psychodrama with trauma survivors: acting out your pain.* London: Jessica Kingsley Publishers.

Burton, J. (1986) *International conflict resolution: theory and practice.* Sussex, England: Wheasheaf Books.

Bustos, D. (1990) "Wenn das Land in der Krise ist, kann man nicht in der Praxis sitzen bleiben." ["When the country is in crisis one cannot remain seated in clinical practice."] *Psychodrama 3,* 30–48.

Bustos, D. (1994) "Locus, matrix, status nascendi and the concept of clusters: wings and roots." In P. Holmes, M. Karp and M. Watson (eds) *Psychodrama since Moreno.* London: Routledge.

Byrne, D. and Clore, G.L. (1970) "A reinforcement model of evaluative responses." *Personality: An International Journal 1,* 103–128.

Carlson-Sabelli, L. (1989) "Role reversal: a concept analysis and reinterpretation of the research literature." *Journal of Group Psychotherapy, Psychodrama and Sociometry 42,* 139–152.

Carson, R.C. (1969) *Interaction concepts of personality.* Chicago, IL: Aldine.

Cartwright, D. and Zander, A. (eds) (1968) *Group dynamics: research and theory,* 2nd edn. New York: Row, Peterson and Co.

Carvalho, E.R and Otero, H.E. (1994) "Sociodrama as a social diagnostic tool: our experience in Paraguay." *Journal of Group Psychotherapy, Psychodrama and Sociometry 46,* 143–149.

Cloke, K. (1993) "Revenge, forgiveness and the magic of mediation." *Mediation Quarterly 11,* 67–78.

Cornelius, H. and Faire, S. (1989) *Everyone can win: how to resolve conflict.* Melbourne: Simon and Schuster.

Covington, C., Williams, P., Arundale, J. and Knox J. (2002) *Terrorism and war: unconscious dynamics of political violence.* London: Karnac.

Cowger, C.G. (1979) "Conflict and conflict management in working with groups." *Social Work with Groups 2,* 309–320.

Crum, T.A. (1976) *The magic of conflict.* New York: Hart.

Cukier, R. (2000) "The psychodrama of mankind: is it really utopian?" *Forum,* 30 October 2002. Available at: http://www.rosacukier.com.br/ingles/artigos1.htm.

Curle A. (1971) *Making peace.* London: Tavistock Publications.

Cushman, P. (1989) "Iron fists–velvet gloves: a study of a mass marathon psychology training." *Psychotherapy 26,* 23–39.

Dajani, K. and Carel, R. (2002) "Neighbors and enemies: lessons to be learned from the Palestinian–Israeli conflict regarding cooperation in public health." *Croatian Medical Journal 43,* 138–140.

Dasberg, H., Davidson, S., Gurlachu, G.L., Filet, B.C. and de Wind, E. (eds) (1987) *Society and trauma of war.* Assen/Maastrich: Van Gorcum.

Davenport, D.S. (1991) "The functions of anger and forgiveness: guidelines for psycho-therapy with victims." *Psychotherapy 28,* 140–144.

De Maré, R., Piper, R. and Thompson, S. (1991) *Koinonia: from hate, through dialogue to culture in the large group.* London: Karnac.

deMause, L. (2002) *The emotional life of nations.* New York: Karnac.

Deutsch, M. (1973) *The resolution of conflict: constructive and destructive processes.* New Haven, CT: Yale University Press.

deVries, M.W. (1996) "Trauma in cultural perspective." In B.A. van der Kolk, A.C. McFarlane and L. Weisaeth (eds) *Traumatic stress.* New York: The Guilford Press.

de Young, M. (1998) "Collective trauma: insights from a research errand." New York: The American Academy of Experts in Traumatic Stress, Inc. Available at: http://www.aaets.org/ article55.htm.

Djuric, Z., Ilić, Z. and Veljkovic, J. (2004) *Psihodrama: Uasopis za grupnu psihoterapiju.* Beograd: Kosmos 1.

Dollard, J., Doob, L., Miller, N., Mowrer, O. and Sears, R. (1939) *Frustration and aggression.* New Haven, CT: Yale University Press.

Donahue, W.A. and Kolt, R. (1993) *Managing interpersonal conflict.* London: Sage.

Doob, L. (1985) "Conflict resolution." In A. Kuper and J. Kuper (eds) *The social science encyclopedia.* London: Routledge and Kegan Paul.

Durkheim, E. (1961) *The elementary forms of the religious life.* London: Barrie and Jenkins.

Durkin, H.E. (1972) "Analytic group therapy and general systems theory." In C.J. Sager and H.S. Kaplan (eds) *Progress in group and family therapy.* New York: Brunner Mazel.

Enright, R.D. and The Human Development Study Group (1996) "Counseling within the forgiveness triad: on forgiving, receiving forgiveness, and self-forgiveness." *Counseling and Values 40*, 107–126.

Erickson, K. (1994) *A new species of trouble: the human experience of modern disasters.* New York: Norton.

Eyerman, R. (2002) *Cultural trauma: slavery and the formation of African-American identity.* Cambridge: Cambridge University Press.

Eysenck, H.I. (1954) *The psychology of politics.* London: Routledge and Kegan Paul.

Ezriel, H. (1973) "Psychoanalytic group therapy." In L.R. Wolberg and E.K. Schwartz (eds) *Group therapy 1973: an overview.* New York: Intercontinental Medical Book Corp.

Fay, M.T., Morrissey, M. and Smyth, M. (1999) *Northern Ireland's troubles: the human costs.* London: Pluto Press.

Feldhendler, D. (1992) *Psychodrama und Theater der Unterdrückten.* Frankfurt: Wilfried Nold.

Feldhendler, D. (1994) "Augusto Boal and Jacob Moreno: theatre and therapy." In M. Schutzman and J. Cohen-Cruz (eds) *Playing Boal.* London and New York: Routledge.

Festinger, L. (1954) "A theory of social comparison processes." *Human Relations 7*, 117–140.

Figley, C.R. (1993) "Introduction." In J.P. Wilson and B. Raphael (eds) *International handbook of traumatic stress syndromes.* New York: Plenum Press.

Figusch, Z. (ed.) (2006) *Sambadrama: the arena of Brazilian psychodrama.* London: Jessica Kingsley Publishers.

Filley, A.C. (1975) *Interpersonal conflict resolution.* Glenview, IL: Scott Foresman.

Fisher, R.J. (1983) "Third party consultation as a method of intergroup conflict resolution: a review of studies." *Journal of Conflict Resolution 27*, 302–334.

Fisher, R.J. and Brown, S. (1988) *Getting together: building a relationship that gets to YES.* Boston, MA: Houghton Mifflin.

Fisher, R.J. and Ury, W. (1981) *Getting to Yes: negotiating agreement without giving in.* Boston, MA: Houghton Mifflin.

Fitzgibbons, R.P. (1986) "The cognitive and emotional uses of forgiveness in the treatment of anger." *Psychotherapy 23*, 629–633.

Fitzgibbons, R. (1998) "Anger and the healing power of forgiveness: a psychiatrist's view." In R. Enright and J. North (eds) *Exploring forgiveness.* Madison, WI: University of Wisconsin Press.

Flugel, J.C. (1945) *Man, morals and society: a psycho-analytical study.* London: Duckworth.

Foa, E.B., Zinbarg, R. and Rothbaum, B.O. (1992) "Uncontrollability and unpredictability in post-traumatic stress disorder: an animal model." *Psychological Bulletin 112*, 218–238.

Folberg, J. and Taylor, A. (1984) *Mediation: a comprehensive guide to resolving conflicts without litigation.* San Francisco, CA: Jossey-Bass.

Foulkes, S.H. (1964) *Therapeutic group analysis.* London: George Allen. Reprinted London: Karnac, 1984.

Fox J. (1994) *Acts of service: spontaneity, commitment, tradition in the nonscripted theatre.* New York: Tusitala Publishing.

Frangsmy, T. (ed.) (1991) *Les Prix Nobel: The Nobel Prizes 1990.* Stockholm: Nobel Foundation.

Frank, J.D. (1967) *Sanity and survival: psychological aspects of war and peace.* New York: Random House.

Freire, P. (1999) *Pedagogy of the oppressed.* New York: The Continuum Publishing Company.

Freud, S. (1930) *Civilization and its discontents. S.E., Vol. 21.* London: Hogarth Press.

Fromm, E. (1962) *Sigmund Freud's mission: an analysis of his personality and influence.* New York: Shimon and Shuster.

Fromm, E. (1973) *The anatomy of human destructiveness.* New York: Holt, Rinehart and Winston.

Galtung, J. (1996) *Peace by peaceful means: peace and conflict, development and civilization.* London: Sage.

Galtung, J. (1998) *Tras la violencia, 3R: reconstruccion, resolucion, reconciliacion.* [*After Violence: 3R, reconstruction, reconciliation, resolution: coping with visible and invisible effects of war and violence.*] Bilbao: Bakeaz/Gernika Gogoratuz. Available at: http://www.transcend.org/TRRECBAS.HTM.

Gampel, Y. (1996) "The interminable uncanny." In L. Rangel and R. Moses-Hrushovski (eds) *Psychoanalysis at the political border.* Madison, CT: International Universities Press.

Gampel, Y. (2000) "Reflections on the prevalence of the uncanny in social violence." In A.C.G.M. Robben and M.M. Suarez-Orozo (eds) *Cultures under siege: collective violence and trauma.* Cambridge: Cambridge University Press.

Gans, J.S. (1989) "Hostility in group psychotherapy." *International Journal of Group Psychotherapy 39*, 499–516.

Gardenswartz, L. and Rowe, A. (1998) *Managing diversity: a complete desk reference and planning guide.* Revised edn. New York: McGraw-Hill.

Geisler, F. (2005) "Wider den egozentrischen Individualismus unserer Tage." ["The egocentric individualism of our time."] In T. Wittinger (ed.) *Handbuch Soziodrama: Die ganze Welt auf der Bühne.* Wiesbaden: VS Verlag für Sozialwissenschaften.

Goffman, E. (1963) *Stigma: notes on the management of spoiled identity.* Englewood Cliffs, NJ: Prentice-Hall.

Gong, S. (2004) *Yi Shu: the art of living with change. Integrating traditional Chinese medicine, psychodrama and the creative arts.* St Louis, MO: Robbins and Sons Press.

Gray, J. (1992) *Men are from Mars, women are from Venus: a practical guide for improving communication and getting what you want in your relationships.* New York: HarperCollins.

Gray, P. and Oliver, K. (eds) (2004) *How shall we remember a trauma? The memory of catastrophe.* Manchester: Manchester University Press.

Haas, R.B. (1948) *Psychodrama and sociodrama in American education.* New York: Beacon House.

Halaby, R. and Sonnenschein, N. (2004) "The Jewish–Palestinian encounter in time of crisis." *Journal of Social Issues 60*, 373–389.

Halaby, R., Sonnenschein, N. and Friedman, A. (2000) "University courses on the Jewish–Arab conflict." In R. Halaby (ed.) *Identities in dialogue: Arab–Jewish encounters in Wahat al-Salam/Neve Shalom.* Tel Aviv: Kibbutz Hameuchad (Hebrew).

Halasz, G. and Kellerman, N. (2005). "Unconditional hate (part 1)." *Mifgashim 5*, 5. [*Also in G. Zygier (ed.) ADC Special Report: a periodic publication of the B'nai B'rith Anti-Defamation Commission Inc.* No. 30, November]

Halling, S. (1994) "Shame and forgiveness." *The Humanistic Psychologist 22*, 74–87.

Hamer, N. (1990) "Group-analytic psychodrama." *Group Analysis 23*, 245–254.

Haney, C.A., Leimer, C. and Lowery, J. (1997) "Spontaneous memorialization: violent death and emerging mourning rituals." *Omega: Journal of Death and Dying 35*, 159–171.

Hare, A.P. (1976) *Handbook of small group research.* 2nd edn New York: Free Press.

Harty, M. and Modell, J. (1991) "The first conflict resolution movement, 1956–1971." *Journal of Conflict Resolution 35*, 720–759.

Haskell, M.R. (1962) "Socioanalysis and psychoanalysis." *Group Psychotherapy 15*, 105–113.

Hayles, R. and Mendez-Russel, A. (1997) *The diversity directive.* Chicago, IL: Irwin Professional Publishing.

Hearst, L. (1993) "Our historical and cultural cargo and its vicissitudes in group analysis." *Group Analysis 26*, 389–405.

Heider, F. (1958) *The psychology of interpersonal relations.* New York: Wiley.

Heitler, S. (1987) "Conflict resolution: a framework for integration." *Journal of Integrative and Eclectic Psychotherapy 6*, 334–350.

Hellinger, B. (2002) *Insights.* Heidelberg: Carl-Auer-Systeme Verlag.

Helmes, J.Y. (1990) *Black and white racial identity: theory, research, and practice.* London: Greenwood Press.

Hess, M. (2004) "Psychodrama und sein Kontext: Gaza April 2004." ["Psychodrama and its context."] *Medico International Schweiz, Bulletin,* 7–8.

Hewstone, M. (1996) "Contact and categorization: social psychological interventions to change intergroup relations." In C.N. Macrae, C. Stangor and M. Hewstone (eds) *Stereotypes and stereotyping.* New York: Guilford.

Hoffman, C. (2002) "The question of evil." August 27 2002. Available at: http://milkriver.blogspot.com/2002_08_01_milkriver_archive.html

Holmgren, M.R. (1993) "Forgiveness and the intrinsic value of persons." *American Philosophical Quarterly 30*, 341–352.

Homans, G.C. (1961) *Social behavior: its elementary forms.* New York: Harcourt, Brace and World.

Hopper, E. (2002) *The social unconscious: selected papers.* London: Jessica Kingsley Publishers.

Hopper, E. (2003) *Traumatic experience in the unconscious life of groups. The fourth basic assumption: incohesion: aggregation/massification or (ba) I:A/M.* London: Jessica Kingsley Publishers.

Horowitz, M.J. (1976) *Stress response syndromes.* New York: Jason Aronson.

Hudgins, M.K. and Drucker, K. (1998) "The containing double as part of the therapeutic spiral model for treating trauma survivors." *The International Journal of Action Methods 51*, 2, 63–74.

Ilic, Z. (2004) "Notes on workshop 'The war in Yugoslavia: searing for answers'." In Z. Djuric, Z. Ilic and J. Veljkovic (eds) *Psihodrama: Casopis za grupnu psihoterapiju.* Beograd: Kosmos.

Janis, I.L. (1972) *Victims of groupthink: a psychological study of foreign-policy decisions and fiascoes.* Boston, MA: Houghton Mifflin.

Janoff-Bulman, R. (1992) *Shattered assumptions: toward a new psychology of trauma.* New York: Free Press.

Johnson, D.R., Feldman, S.C., Lubin, H. and Soutwick, S.M. (1995) "The therapeutic use of ritual and ceremony in the treatment of post-traumatic stress disorder." *Journal of Traumatic Stress 8*, 2, 283–291.

Johnson, D.W. and Dustin, R. (1970) "The initiation of cooperation through role reversal." *Journal of Social Psychology 82*, 193–203.

Johnson, J.T. (1981) *The just war tradition and the restraint of war.* Princeton, NJ: Princeton University Press.

Johnson, J.T. (1987) *The quest for peace.* Princeton, NJ: Princeton University Press.

Jung, C.G. (1953) *Collected works.* New York: Pantheon Books.

Kalayjian, A., Shahinian, S.P., Gergerian, E.L. and Saraydarian, L. (1996) "Coping with Ottoman Turkish genocide: exploration of the experience of Armenian survivors." *Journal of Traumatic Stress 9*, 87–97.

Karp, M. (2000) "Zerka Moreno: an interview." *The International Forum of Group Psychotherapy 8*, 27–32.

Kaufman, E. (1996) *Innovative problem solving: a model program/workshop.* University of Maryland, Monograph No.7. Center for International Development and Conflict Management.

Kaul, T.J. and Bednar, R.I. (1986) "Experiential group research." In S. Garfield and A. Bergin (eds) *Handbook of psychotherapy and behavior change*, 3rd edn. New York: Wiley.

Kayat, C. (1981) *Mohammed Cohen.* Paris: Editions du Seuil.

Kellermann, P.F. (1992) *Focus on psychodrama.* London: Jessica Kingsley Publishers.

Kellermann, P.F. (1996) "Interpersonal conflict management in group psychotherapy: an integrative perspective." *Group Analysis 29*, 257–275.

Kellermann, P.F. (1998) "Sociodrama." *Group Analysis 31*, 179–195. Portuguese Translation: *Revista Brasileira de Psicodrama 6*, 2, 1998, 51–68. Swedish Translation: Berglind, H. (ed.) *Skapande Ögonblick.* Stockholm: Cura, 1998, 40–53. Russian Translation: *Psychodrama and modern psychotherapy.* Ukraine 4, 2004, 7–21. German Translation: Wittinger, T. (2005) (ed.) *Handbuch Soziodrama: Die ganze Welt auf der Bühne.* Wiesbaden: VS Verlag für Sozialwissenschaften.

Kellermann, P.F. (2000) "The therapeutic aspects of psychodrama with traumatized people." In P.F. Kellermann and K. Hudgins (eds) *Psychodrama with trauma survivors: acting out your pain.* London: Jessica Kingsley Publishers.

Kellermann, N.P.F. (2001a) "The long-term psychological effects and treatment of Holocaust trauma." *Journal of Loss and Trauma 6*, 197–218.

Kellermann, N.P.F. (2001b) "Transmission of Holocaust trauma: an integrative view." *Psychiatry: Interpersonal and Biological Processes 64*, 3, 256–267.

Kellermann, N.P.F. (2001c) "Psychopathology in children of Holocaust survivors: a review of the research literature." *Israel Journal of Psychiatry 38*, 36–46.

Kellermann, N.P.F. (2001d) "Perceived parental rearing behavior in children of Holocaust survivors." *Israel Journal of Psychiatry 38*, 58–68.

Kellermann, N.P.F. (2004) *Zur Auseinandersetzung mit dem Nationalsozialismus in Österreich.* [*Facing the Holocaust in Austria*]. Unpublished manuscript.

Kellermann, N.P.F. (2005) "Unconditional hate: anti-Semitism in the contemporary world." *The Jewish Magazine 91*, June 2005. Available at: http://www.jewishmag.com/91mag/antisemitism/antisemitism.htm.

Kellermann, P.F. and Hudgins, K. (eds) (2000) *Psychodrama with trauma survivors: acting out your pain.* London: Jessica Kingsley Publishers.

Kester, J.D. (2001) "From eyewitness testimony to health care to post-genocide healing successes and surprises in the application of psychological science." *APS Observer Online 14*, 6 (July/August). Washington, DC: Association for Pychological Science. Available at: http://www.psychologicalscience.org/observer/ 0701/pressymp.html.

Kibel, H. and Stein, A. (1981) "The group-as-a-whole approach: an appraisal." *International Journal of Group Psychotherapy 31*, 409–427.

King Jr, M.L. (1967) *Massey Lecture no. 5: A Christmas Sermon on Peace.* Atlanta, GA: MWC. Sound cassette: analog. 671224–000.

Klain, E. (1992) "Experiences and perspectives of an individual in the war in Croatia (1991/1992)." *Croatian Medical Journal 33*, 4, 3–13.

Klain, E. (1998) "Intergenerational aspects of the conflict in the former Yugoslavia." In Y. Danieli (ed.) *International handbook of multigenerational legacies of trauma.* New York: Plenum Press.

Klein, E.B. (1993) "Large groups in treatment and training settings." *Group 17*, 198–209.

Knepler, A.E. (1970) "Sociodrama in public affairs." *Group Psychotherapy and Psychodrama 13*, 127–134.

Kreeger, L. (ed.) (1975) *The large group: dynamics and therapy.* Itasca, IL: Peacock.

Kressel, N.J. (1993) *Political psychology: classic and contemporary readings.* New York: Paragon House.

Leary, T. (1957) *Interpersonal diagnosis of personality.* New York: Roland.

LeBon, G. (1896) *The crowd: a study of the popular mind.* New York: The Macmillan Co. Available at: http://etext.virginia.edu/toc/modeng/public/BonCrow.html.

Lemert, E. (1951) *Social pathology.* New York: McGraw-Hill.

Lensky, G. (1966) *Power and privilege.* New York: McGraw-Hill.

Lewin, K. (1948) *Resolving social conflicts: selected papers on group dynamics.* New York: Harper.

Lewin, K. (1951) *Field theory in social science: selected theoretical papers by Kurt Lewin.* New York: Atarper.

Leutz, G. (1991) "Moreno 'in Fahrt'." [Moreno on the way.] *Psychodrama 4*, 2, 169–172.

Lindner, E.G. (2001) "Humiliation – trauma that has been overlooked: an analysis based on fieldwork in Germany, Rwanda/Burundi, and Somalia." *Traumatology 7*, 1, 51–79.

Lindner, E.G. (2002) "Healing the cycles of humiliation: how to attend to the emotional aspects of 'unsolvable' conflicts and the use of 'humiliation entrepreneurship'." *Peace and Conflict: Journal of Peace Psychology 8*, 2, 125–139.

Lobeck, G. (1990) "Psychodrama-ausbildung in der DDR: Erlebnisbericht über eine deutsch–deutsch begegnung" ["Psychodrama in the German Democratic Republic: Some experiences of a German–German encounter"]. *Psychodrama 3*, 23–29.

Luce, R.D. and Raiffa, H. (1957) *Games and decisions.* New York: Wiley.

Mackay, C. (1841) *Extraordinary popular delusions and the madness of crowds.* New Edition: New York: Random House (1980).

Macrae, C.N., Stangor, C. and Hewstone, M. (eds) (1996) *Stereotypes and stereotyping.* New York: Guilford.

Main, T. (1975) "Some psychodynamics of large groups." In L. Kreeger (ed.) *The large group: dynamics and therapy.* Itasca, IL: Peacock.

Manson, S., Beals, J., O'Nell, T., Piasecki, J. *et al.* (1996) "Wounded spirits, ailing hearts: PTSD and related disorders among American Indians." In A.K. Marsella, M.J. Friedman, E.T. Gerrity and R.S. Scurfield (eds) *Ethnocultural aspects of post-traumatic stress disorder.* Washington, DC: American Psychological Association Press.

Marineau, R.F. (1989) *Jacob Levy Moreno 1889–1974.* International Library of Group Psychotherapy and Group Process. London and New York: Tavistock/Routledge.

Maslow, A.H. (1977) "Politics 3." *Journal of Humanistic Psychology 17*, 5–20.

McCann, I.L. and Pearlman, L.A. (1990) *Psychological trauma and the adult survivor: theory, therapy and transformation.* New York: Brunner/Mazel.

McCullough, M.E., Pargament, K.I. and Thoresen, C.E. (eds) (2000) *Forgiveness: theory, research and practice.* New York: Guilford Press.

McDougall, W. (1920) *The group mind.* New York: Putnam.

Merton, R.K. (1968) *Social theory and social structure.* New York: The Free Press.

Milgram, S. and Toch, H. (1969) "Collective behavior: crowds and social movements." In *The handbook of social psychology* 2nd edn, Vol. 4. Reading, MA: Addison-Wesley.

Miller, E.J. and Rice, A.K. (1967) *Systems of organization.* London: Tavistock.

Mindell, A. (1995) *Sitting in the fire: large group transformation using conflict and diversity.* Portland, OR: Lao Tse Press.

Mitchell J. (1983) "When disaster strikes: the critical incident stress debriefing process." *Journal of Emergency Medical Services 8,* 36–39.

Mitchell, J. and Everly, G.S. (2001) *Critical incident stress debriefing: an operations manual.* 3rd edn. Ellicott City, MD: Chevron Publishing Corporation.

Moore, B.E. and Fine, B.D. (eds) (1990) *Psychoanalytic terms and concepts.* New Haven, CT: Yale University Press.

Moreno, J.L. (1943/1972) "The concept of sociodrama: a new approach to the problem of inter-cultural relations." *Sociometry 6,* 434–449. (Also in J.L. Moreno (1972) *Psychodrama, Vol. 1.* New York: Beacon House).

Moreno, J.L. (1953) *Who shall survive?* New York: Beacon House.

Moreno, J.L. (1972) *Psychodrama, Vol. 1.* New York: Beacon House.

Moreno, J.L. and Moreno, Z.T. (1969) *Psychodrama, Vol. 3.* New York: Beacon House.

Moreno, Z.T. (2006) The quintessential Zerka: writings by Zerka Toeman Moreno on pychodrama, sociometry and group pychotherapy. London: Routledge.

Morris, D. (1969) *In the human zoo.* London: McGraw-Hill.

Moyer, K.E. (1968) "Kinds of aggression and their physiological basis." *Communications in Behavioral Biology 2,* 65–87.

Netherlands Medical Society (1939) *Committee on war 'prophylaxis'.* Amsterdam: Elsevier.

Nisbett, R. and Ross, L. (1980) *Human inference: strategies and shortcomings of social judgment.* Englewood Cliffs, NJ: Prentice-Hall.

North, J. (1987) "Wrongdoing and forgiveness." *Philosophy 62,* 499–508.

O'Byrne, M. (2005) "A review of cross-cultural training in mental health." Montreal, Quebec: McGill. Available at: http://www.mcgill.ca/ccs/report/appendices/review.

Ochberg, F.M. (1988) *Post-traumatic therapy and victims of violence.* New York: Brunner/Mazel.

O'Connor, T. (1989) "Therapy for a dying planet: we are the cause. We are the cure." Reprinted in *The evolving therapist: the family therapy network.* Washington and New York: Guilford.

Okey, J.L. (1992) "Human aggression: the etiology of individual differences." *Humanistic Psychology 32,* 51–64.

Orlick, T. (1982) *The second co-operative sports and games handbook.* New York: Pantheon.

Ormont, L.R. (1984) "The leader's role in dealing with aggression in groups." *International Journal of Group Psychotherapy 34,* 553–572.

Parson, E. (1985) "Ethnicity and traumatic stress." In C.R. Figley (ed.) *Trauma and its wake.* New York: Brunner/Mazel.

Parson, E. (1990) "Post-traumatic psychocultural therapy (PTpsyCT): integration of trauma and shattering social labels of the self." *Journal of Contemporary Psychotherapy 20,* 237–258.

Parsons, T. (1967) *Sociological theory and modern society.* New York: Free Press.

Perry, B.D. (1999) "Memories of fear: transgenerational memory of culture and society." In J. Goodwin and R. Attias (eds) *Splintered reflections: images of the body in trauma.* New York: Basic Books. Available at: http://www.childtrauma.org/ctamaterials/memories.asp.

Petzold, G.H. and Mathias, U. (1982) *Rollenentwicklung und Identitet [Role development identity].* Paderborn: Junfermann.

Pines, M. (1988) "Mediation papers: a group-analytic response." *Group Analysis 21,* 57–59.

Powell, A. (1986) "A conference success: psychodrama and group analysis are compatible." *Group Analysis 19,* 63–65.

Powell, A. (1989) "The nature of the matrix." *Group Analysis 22,* 271–281.

Powell, A. (1994) "Toward a unifying concept of the group matrix." In D. Brown and L. Linkin (eds) *The psyche and the social world.* London: Routledge.

Pruitt, D. and Rubin, J. (1986) *Social conflict: escalation, stalemate and settlement.* New York: Random House.

Public Papers of the Presidents of the United States. (1997) *Book 2: William J. Clinton: July 1–December 31.* Washington, DC: United States Government Printing.

Pyszczynski, T., Solomon, S. and Greenberg, J. (2003) *In the wake of 9/11: the psychology of terror.* Washington, DC: American Psychological Association Press.

Rapoport, R.N. (1988) "Mediation and group analysis: creating an interface." *Group Analysis 21,* 3–8.

Rice, A.K. (1965) *Learning for leadership.* London: Tavistock.

Robins, R.S. and Post, J.M. (1997) *Political paranoia: the psychopolitics of hatred.* New Haven and London: Yale University Press.

Rogers, C.R. (1965) "Dealing with psychological tensions." *Journal of Applied Behavioral Science 1,* 6–29.

Rose, M. (1998) *Fighting for peace.* London: Harvill Press.

Rosenberg, M. (2000). *Nonviolent communication: a language of compassion.* Encihitas, CA: Puddle Dancer Press.

Rothman, J. (1992) *From confrontation to cooperation: resolving ethnic and regional conflict.* Newbury Park, CA: Sage.

Rubin, J.Z. (1980) "Experimental research on third-party interventions in conflict: toward some generalizations." *Psychological Bulletin 87,* 379–381.

Rubin, T.I. (1969) *The angry book.* London: Collier-Macmillan.

Rummel, R.J. (1975–1981) *Understanding conflict and war.* Beverly Hills, CA: Sage.

Rummel R.J. (1997) "Is collective violence correlated with social pluralism?" *Journal of Peace Research 34,* 163–175.

Rutan, J.S., Alonso, A. and Groves, J.E. (1988) "Understanding defenses in group psychotherapy." *International Journal of Group Psychotherapy 38,* 459–472.

Sabelli, H. (1990) *Process theory of peace.* Chicago, IL: Society for the Advancement of Clinical Philosophy.

Scheff, T.J. (1994) *Bloody revenge: emotion, nationalism and war.* Boulder,CO: Westview Press (2nd edn by iUniverse, 2000).

Scheff, T.J. (2004) "Comments on Blind Trust by Vamik Volkan." *PsychCritique.* Available at: http://www.humiliationstudies.org/news/archives/000168.html.

Schermer, V.L. and Pines, M. (eds) (1994) *Ring of fire: primitive affect and object relations in group psychotherapy.* London: Routledge.

Schneider, S. and Weinberg, H. (eds) (2003) *The large-group revisited: the herd, primal horde, crowds and masses*. London: Jessica Kingsley Publishers.

Schutz, W. (1973) *Elements of encounter*. Big Sur, CA: Joy Press.

Schützenberger, A. (2000) "Health and death: hidden links through the family tree." In P.F. Kellermann and M.K. Hudgins (eds) *Psychodrama with trauma survivors*. London: Jessica Kingsley Publishers.

Scobie, E.D. and Scobie, G.E.W. (1998) "Damaging events: the perceived need for forgiveness." *Journal for the Theory of Social Behaviour 28*, 373–401.

Scurfield, R.M. (1985) "Post-trauma stress assessment and treatment: overview and formulations." In C.R. Figley (ed.) *Trauma and its wake, Vol. 1*. New York: Brunner/Mazel.

Seel, R. (2001) "Anxiety and incompetence in the large group: a psychodynamic perspective." *Journal of Organizational Change Management 14*, 5, 493–504.

Sharp, G. (1973) *The politics of nonviolent action*. Manchester, NH: Extending Horizons Books.

Sharp, G. (2005) *Waging nonviolent struggle: 20th century practice and 21st century potential*. Manchester, NH: Extending Horizons Books.

Shaw, M.E. (1976) *Group dynamics: the psychology of small group behavior*. New York: McGraw-Hill

Shay, J. (1994) *Achilles in Vietnam: combat trauma and the undoing of character*. London: Touchstone Books.

Sherif, M. and Sherif, C. (1969) *Social psychology*. New York: Harper.

Sholevar, G.P. (1981) *The handbook of marriage and marital therapy*. New York: Medical and Scientific Books.

Simmel, E.C., Hahn, M.E. and Walters, J.K. (1983) *Aggressive behavior: a genetic and neural approach*. Hillsdale, NJ: Erlbaum.

Simon Jr., W.E. (2005) *On becoming American: reasserting citizenship in the immigration debate*. Heritage Lecture No. 890, July 21. Available at: http://heritage.org/research/politicalphilosophy/h1890.cfm.

Slaikeu, K.A. (1996) *When push comes to shove: a practical guide to mediating disputes*. San Francisco, CA: Jossey-Bass.

Smedes, L.B. (1984) *Forgive and forget: healing the hurts we don't deserve*. New York: Harper and Row.

Smith, T.W. (1992) "Hostility and health: current status of a psychosomatic hypothesis." *Health Psychology 11*, 139–150.

Sobel, J. (1983) *Everybody wins: 393 noncompetitive games*. New York: Walker and Co.

Solotowitzki, R. (2004) "Social drama and sociodrama." *Psychodrama and modern psychotherapy 4*, 4–6: The Kiev Psychodrama Association (Russian).

Sprague, K. (1998) "Permission to interact: a who, how and why of sociodrama." In M. Karp, P. Holmes and K. Bradshaw Tauvon (eds) *The handbook of psychodrama*. London: Routledge.

Staub, E. (1989) *The roots of evil: the origins of genocide and other group violence*. New York: Cambridge University Press.

Staub, E. and Pearlman, L.A. (2001) "Healing, reconciliation and forgiving after genocide and other collective violence." In G.Raymond, S.J. Helmick and R.L Petersen (eds) *Forgiveness and reconciliation: religion, public policy, and conflict transformation*. Philadelphia: Templeton Foundation Press.

Stein, S.A., Ingersoll, R.E. and Treadwell, T.W. (1995) "Sociodrama and professional/ethical conflicts." *Journal of Group Psychotherapy, Psychodrama and Sociometry 48*, 31–41.

Sternberg, P. and Garcia, A. (1989) *Sociodrama: who's in your shoes?* New York: Praeger (2nd edn, 2000).

Stossel, S. (2001) "Terror TV." *The American prospect online 12,* 18, October 22 2001. Available at: http://prospect.org/print/V12/18/stossel-s.html.

Suedfeld, P. (1997) "Reactions to societal trauma: distress and/or stress." *Political Psychology 18*, 849–861.

Sunstein, C.R. (1999) "The law of group polarization." University of Chicago Law School. *John M. Olin Law and Economics Working Paper 91.* Available at: http://ssrn.com/abstract=199668.

Tajfel, H. (1981) *Human groups and social categories.* Cambridge: Cambridge University Press.

Tajfel, H. and Turner, J. (1986) "An integrative theory of inter-group conflict." In W.G. Austen and S. Worchel (eds) *Psychology of inter-group relations.* Monterey, CA: Brooks Cole.

Tauber, C.D. (2004) "Recent developments in the Balkans and the coalition for work with pschodrama and peace." *Nonviolent Change Journal 18*, 2. Available at: http://circlepoint.org/ncarticle0601.html.

Tavris, C. (1983) "Anger defused." *Psychology Today 16*, 25–35.

Taylor, D.M. and Moghaddam, F.M. (1987) *Theories of intergroup relations: international social psychological perspectives.* New York: Praeger.

Triandis, H., Brislin, R. and Hui C.H. (1988) "Cross cultural training across the individualism–collectivism divide." *International Journal of Intercultural Relations 12*, 269–289.

Turner, V. (1967) *The forest of symbols.* Ithaca, New York: Cornell.

Tutu, D. (2000) *On the Truth and Reconciliation Commission.* Johannesburg: University of the Witswatersrand. Available at: http://www.wits.ac.za/histp/tutu_quotes_by.htm#trc.

Van den Bout, J., Havenaar, J.M. and Meijler-Iljina, L.I. (1995) "Health problems in areas contaminated by the Chernobyl disaster." In R.J. Kleber, C.R. Figley and B.P.R. Gersons (eds) *Beyond trauma: cultural and societal dynamics.* New York: Plenum.

van Tongeren, P., Brenk, M., Hellema, M. and Verhoeven, J. (2005) *People building peace II.* Boulder, CO: Lynne Rienner Publishers.

Verzberger, Y. (1990) *The world in their minds: information processing, cognition and perception in foreign policy decision-making.* Stanford, CA: Stanford University Press.

Verzberger, Y. (1997) "The antinomies of collective political trauma: a pre-theory." *Political Psychology 18*, 4, 863–876.

Volkan, V. (1988) *The need to have enemies and allies: from clinical practice to international relationships.* Northvale, NJ: Jason Aronson.

Volkan, V. (1991) "On chosen trauma." *Mind and Human Interaction 3*, 13.

Volkan, V. (1992) "Ethnonationalistic rituals: an introduction." *Mind and Human Interaction 4*, 3–19.

Volkan, V. (1997) *Bloodlines: from ethnic pride to ethnic terrorism.* New York: Farrar, Straus and Giroux.

Volkan, V. (1999) "The tree model: a comprehensive psychopolitical approach to unofficial diplomacy and the reduction of ethnic tension." *Mind and Human Interaction 10*, 142–210.

Volkan, V. (2001) "September 11 and societal regression." *Mind and Human Interaction 12*, 196–216.

Volkan, V. (2002) "Large-group identity: border psychology and related societal processes." *Keynote address at the German Psychoanalytic Association annual meeting May 10 2002, in Leipzig, Germany.* Charlottesville, VA: University of Virginia. Available at: http://www.healthsystem.virginia.edu/internet/csmhi/vol13volkan.cfm

Volkan, V. (2004) *Blind trust: large groups and their leaders in times of crises and terror.* Charlottesville, VA: Pitchstone Publishing.

Volkan, V. and Itzkowitz, N. (1994) *Turks and Greeks: neighbors in conflict.* Cambridgeshire, England: Eothen Press.

Volkas, A. (2002) "Healing the wounds of history." *Keynote speech delivered to the National Association for Drama Therapy, November 9, in Albuquerque, New Mexico.* San Francisco: The Center for the Living Arts. Available at: http://www.livingartscenter.org.

Walters, R.P. (1981) *Anger: yours, mine and what to do about it.* Grand Rapids, MI: Zondervan.

Walton, R.E. (1969) *Interpersonal peacemaking: confrontations and third party consultation.* Reading, MA: Addison-Wesley.

Wessells, M.G. and Monteiro, C. (2000) "Healing wounds of war in Angola: a community-based approach." In D. Donald, A. Dawes and J. Louw (eds) *Addressing childhood adversity.* Cape Town: David Philip.

Whitaker, D.M. and Lieberman, M.A. (1964) *Psychotherapy through the group process.* New York: Atherton Press.

Wiener, R. (1997) *Creative training: sociodrama and team building.* London: Jessica Kingsley Publishers.

Wiener, R. (2001) "Changing the world: or at least a little bit." *The British Journal of Psychodrama and Sociodrama 16,* 115–118.

Williams, D. (2001) *Power or peace? Trauma, change and psychoanalogical climate in national and international affairs – 2001.* Woking, Surrey: Eos Life Work. Available at: http://www.eoslifework.co.uk/pop1.html.

Wittinger, T. (ed.) (2005) *Handbuch Soziodrama: Die ganze Welt auf der Bühne.* [*Handbook sociodrama: the whole world on the stage*]. Wiesbaden: VS Verlag für Sozialwissenschaften.

Wolpert, S. (1991) *India.* Los Angeles, CA: University of California Press.

Woodhouse, T. (ed.) (1991) *Peacemaking in a troubled world.* New York: St. Martins Press.

Yalom, I.D. (1975) *The theory and practice of group psychotherapy.* 2nd revised edn. New York: Basic Books.

Zichy, L. (1990) "Psychodrama in der Perestroika: Ungarn im Wandel." ["Psychodrama in the perestroika: Hungary in change"] *Psychodrama 3,* 3–21.

Zuretti, M. (1994) "The Co-Unconscious." In P. Holmes, M. Karp and M. Watson (eds) *Psychodrama since Moreno.* London: Routledge.

Zuretti, M. (2001) "Sociopsychodrama." *The British Journal of Psychodrama and Sociodrama 16,1,* 111–114.

Zuretti, M. (2005) *Personal Communication.*

Subject Index

Author Index